COMING TO CONSENSUS

Coming to Consensus

A Case Study for the Churches

Jill Tabart

Risk
BOOK SERIES

WCC Publications, Geneva

Cover design: Rob Lucas
Cover photo: WCC/Peter Williams

ISBN 2-8254-1392-5

World Council of Churches
150 route de Ferney, P.O. Box 2100
1211 Geneva 2, Switzerland
Web site: http://www.wcc-coe.org

No. 103 in the Risk Book Series

Printed in Switzerland

Table of Contents

Foreword

How do Christians reach decisions together? How do councils of the church local, regional, national, ecumenical best work their way towards a policy resolution? How can the church reach an agreed outcome, so that like the apostles at the council of Jerusalem we can say "it has seemed good to the Holy Spirit and to us to..." (Acts 15:28)?

This book by Australian church leader Jill Tabart is a very timely contribution to the study of these questions. It tells how the Uniting Church in Australia has grappled with the issue of Christian decision-making, and how other bodies like the World Alliance of Reformed Churches and the World Council of Churches are moving now in similar directions.

Jill is a medical practitioner who served as a president of the Uniting Church from 1994 to 1997. She is regarded in Australia as the most knowledgeable person in the consensus method and as our best moderator of a council meeting using consensus procedures.

In 2002 the Special Commission on Orthodox Participation in the WCC proposed that the WCC move to a consensus method of decision-making. It sparked a spirited discussion in the central committee. Protestants are well used to Western parliamentary procedures and know how to apply them to help win an argument. Some of them feared consensus would mean "lowest-common-denominator" decisions, ducking of hard issues, and allowing a minority to exercise a veto. I remember speaking reassuringly to the central committee out of my experience in the Uniting Church, where we have found our consensus procedures enable more voices to be heard, create more respectful listening and deeper trust in one another, and bring about better decisions. Similar fears held by some of the most astute council members in the UCA before we moved to consensus have proved, I believe, to be groundless.

Moving from a parliamentary model to a consensus model has markedly changed the ethos of Uniting Church meetings. Council members have turned away from primarily wanting to win an argument towards wanting to engage in a discernment process where the will of God is sought through a careful process of listening and responding to one another. Making decisions by consensus is far more fruitful than the old adversarial approach, both in terms of decisions and relationships.

Of course, the consensus method adopted in Australia is not perfect. It is transferable to other churches, but it will need adapting to fit different contexts.

It is most encouraging that various churches across the world are now addressing the question of decision-making processes. In Scandinavia, in North America, in southern Africa, in New Zealand, churches are working on alternatives to the old parliamentary processes. They are asking what is the most Christian method of decision-making for church councils. It is a challenge for every church. For ecumenical councils it is an even bigger challenge. Developing a consensus method to serve meetings where vastly different church traditions are represented will be a very complex venture. Considerable training will be required, both for council members and for moderators.

In the appendices to this book you will find two charts of the Uniting Church's procedures. The first shows how the consensus procedures work. Do not be deterred by what at first glance looks exceedingly complex! In practice only the most controversial issues will require all the possible steps shown on the flow chart. The second chart illustrates the backstop position of formal majority procedures. These are the traditional parliamentary procedures which can still be employed in the Uniting Church if consensus cannot be reached and if 75 percent of council members believe it is essential that a decision must be made at that meeting.

Also in the appendices you will find the Consensus Decision-making section of the report of the Special Commission. This was largely written by Commission member D'Arcy Wood, who preceded Jill Tabart in 1997 as president of the Uniting Church. It outlines the way in which the consensus method is to be followed by the WCC central committee and the WCC assembly, from 2005 onwards.

The *Manual for Meetings in the Uniting Church in Australia* gives complete information about the Uniting

Church's procedures. It can be downloaded from the web-page http://nat.uca.org.au/regulations/2001/index.htm, and you will need Adobe Acrobat to read it.

After a few hundred years of following parliamentary procedures in Protestant churches, it is high time we Christians looked seriously at how we make decisions together. I am confident a consensus model of decision-making will equip churches and the ecumenical movement to discern God's will more clearly. Enjoy and learn from this book, as you work in your church towards more appropriate methods of Christian decision-making.

Gregor Henderson
General Secretary,
Uniting Church in Australia, 1989-2000
Uniting Church president-elect 2003-2006
Member, WCC central committee, 1998-

1. When Did It Begin?

It was one of those rare insights that turns out to be a defining moment for future change. At the time you think it's insignificant or at most perhaps an intriguing suggestion, but in retrospect you think, "Was this one of those kairos moments – the Spirit's leading, God's timing?"

The fifth national assembly of the Uniting Church in Australia, which convened in Melbourne, Victoria, in May 1988, resolved to ask a small task group to look at the standing orders and rules of debate. In preparing for that assembly meeting, the business committee had become aware of the need for some revision work, and had brought this recommendation as part of their routine report to the assembly. Basically, the purpose was to tidy up a number of discrepancies, because the rules contained some ambiguities that seemed to hinder the flow of a meeting. An ordinary enough resolution, one might think, and there were certainly many participants in that assembly who silently gave thanks that someone else would be named for this boring – although necessary – mundane work of revising regulations.

That resolution became the modest starting-point for change of a magnitude undreamed of at the time. The small group of experienced church-meeting participants and business committee gurus who agreed to take on the task became (inadvertently) the channel for a Holy Spirit-inspired change. It was out of this process that the young Australian church embarked on its remarkable journey into consensus decision-making.

The Uniting Church in Australia was just eleven years old in 1988. Three denominations of Reformed and Evangelical persuasion – the Congregational Union of Australia, the Methodist Church of Australasia and the Presbyterian Church of Australia – had come into union in 1977. This momentous event had occurred only after decades of prayerful persistence, visionary verve and careful collaboration. The passion for unity was driven by the prayer of Jesus found in chapter 17 of John's gospel, "that they may all be one... so that the world may believe...", and born out of the conviction, underlined in the very first paragraph of the Basis of

Union, that unity is "both Christ's gift and will for the church".

It was apparent right from the inauguration of the new church that the concept of unity was not meant to be limited to continuing conversations with other denominations. (Choosing the name "The *Uniting* Church in Australia", implying ongoing activity, was a deliberate declaration that the process of uniting the body of Christ is far from complete. The name itself signifies a prophetic promise to persevere on the ecumenical pathway towards wider church unity.)

Careful consideration of the basis of union on which the Uniting Church was formed makes it clear that seeking unity was also expected to be the manner in which governance responsibilities would be fulfilled. The church was to recognize that "responsibility for government in the church belongs to the people of God by virtue of the gifts and tasks which God has laid upon them". It was to acknowledge "that Christ alone is supreme in his church, and that he may speak to it through any of its councils". What's more, the basis of union declares that it is "the task of every council to wait upon God's word, and to obey God's will in the matters allocated to its oversight". Each council would "recognize the limits of its own authority and give heed to other councils of the church, so that the whole body of believers may be united by mutual submission in the service of the gospel".

Stirring sentiments and wise words – but even so, old habits do have the propensity to die hard!

There were standing orders and rules of debate included in the regulations of the new church, under the section heading "Government and Administration". Along with most churches with origins in Europe, the three churches that came into union had been accustomed to adversarial style debate and decision-making in their meeting structure, patterned on the Westminster parliamentary system. That model had been accepted unquestioningly as the way to proceed in most Australian institutions, not just the churches. The fact that motions could validly be passed by just one more than fifty percent of those voting did not seem to detract from an understanding that the church had spoken in the resultant decision. Any disquiet felt by those who strongly opposed an outcome was expected to be subdued for the sake of unity in the church, and out of respect for the authority of the particular council.

These difficulties were compounded by the fact that the Uniting Church's standing orders and rules of debate were largely an amalgamation of procedures employed by each of the former denominations – and those denominations had each developed their own tradition in interpreting the procedures. A phrase in these orders and rules was not necessarily interpreted in the same way by everyone, but might be influenced by the experience of one's former church tradition.

It should not have been surprising, therefore, that contentious issues had in effect (if not always overtly) often polarized the church – and of course its preceding separate denominations – over many years. It should not have been surprising that broad ownership by church members of the outcome in a debate was often not evident, after a representative council had determined a particular stance for the church.

It should not have been surprising that the time was ripe for the emergence of another way to reach decisions in the councils of the church!

2. What Was Wrong with the Tried and True?

At the first meeting of the task group set up by the 1988 assembly, the scope of their work was considered. It was a cold, uncompromising minute that set the agenda: *To review the standing orders and rules of debate and, after consultation with the legal reference committee, to recommend appropriate amendments to the standing committee for presentation to the next assembly.*

Almost casually, it seems, as the convenor drew up an agenda for that first meeting, a question arose about the unique nature of the church as a faith community. What difference might such self-understanding make in decision-making, compared with secular and business organizations? Were the present standing orders to be the starting point for the task group's work? Was the process to begin merely by identifying gaps and inconsistencies in what was an already familiar way of conducting business? Or could the task group start with a clean slate, giving thought to the underlying purpose of meeting procedure for councils of the church?

To consider going back to more fundamental factors in honouring the intent of the resolution was no flippant tangential approach, raised idly. These members of the task group were people who knew the rules of debate well, who all had wide knowledge and experience in the tried and true structures of meeting procedure. They all appreciated the fairness of majority rule, and the ordered approach in dealing with contentious matters. They valued the strong tradition of oratorical persuasion in considering issues. They relished the cut-and-thrust of well-informed debate, and affirmed the just process in the parliamentary system which allows for a minority of two to be able to raise an issue (the mover and seconder of a motion or an amendment). They recognized that it was out of this rich traditional background of experience in meeting practice and decision-making that the Uniting Church in Australia had emerged. However, they doubted if tinkering with amendments to the traditional procedures would address the underlying concerns.

Was it perhaps the wrong question they were being asked to address? So was born the idea of delving deeper, of starting with a broader canvas on which to develop the task group's work.

How procedures have developed through the ages...

No one disputes that adversarial procedures have a long and valued history. They arose in forums for intellectual debate in Greece and Rome, from a time before the birth of Christ. Their formalized structure was appropriate for the disciplined exploration of philosophical issues, which was a popular form of public entertainment at the time. They influenced the functioning of councils of the church in the early centuries of the Christian era, offering an ordered way of dealing with contentious issues. And something of the concept of adversarial procedures had arrived in England with the Roman invasion. However, it was not until the Model Parliament, summoned by Edward I in 1295, that anything resembling the beginning of order in public governance could be recognized on those foreign shores far from Rome and Athens.

But procedures cultivated progressively in the Middle Ages, to address the need for order and structure in a two-party English parliamentary system, do not necessarily retain an ageless global relevance. Their development at the time certainly contributed to an almost miraculous turn-around from chaos to stability in the way in which England was governed. A sense of dignity and decorum and fairness had been markedly absent in the English system, prior to the first formal statement of proceedings in the House of Commons, Sir Thomas Smyth's *Lex Republica Anglorum,* when that was codified in 1583. This forerunner of an enduring parliamentary debating system established adversarial, majority-rule procedures as the unquestioned norm for four hundred years throughout the English-speaking world.[1]

It should have come as no surprise to anyone, however, to realize that circumstances and needs might be different on the other side of the world at the end of the 20th century, for

---

[1] *Encylopedia Britannica* 9:162.

a new Australian church seeking to be true to the guidance of the Holy Spirit in discerning God's will for the way forward.

Already in the decade-long life of the Uniting Church there was evidence of tough issues dividing opinion within the church. And there was something of that disquiet in the memory of those who had held responsibilities in the former denominations prior to 1977. But while a pronouncement by a particular council of the church may have engendered a grumbling reaction by some in the past, it seems that mostly there had been a culture of submissive acceptance of decisions by those in authority. That attitude had also been reflected in a passive expectation that "someone else" would take responsibility for advocacy or implementation of the outcome on a divisive issue. Wide ownership – or even accurate knowledge – of important decisions of councils of the church had been far from universal amongst the total church membership.

By the 1980s, increasingly easier communications were beginning to result in a more informed membership of the church. And there was a growing interest in the expectation expressed in the basis of union that all members have a responsibility to contribute in the life of the congregation. "[The Uniting Church] acknowledges with thanksgiving that the one Spirit has endowed the members of Christ's church with a diversity of gifts, and that there is no gift without its corresponding service: all ministries have a part in the ministry of Christ." Increasingly, congregations were expecting elected councils to be explicitly accountable to the bodies from which the representative membership was drawn. Contentious matters might well be the topic of conversation far beyond the closed doors of councils. Decisions needing merely a simple majority to pass may have carried all the weight of a council's imprimatur, yet they could leave a significant minority of that council (and presumably of the whole church membership) disenfranchized in the resultant decision to be enacted by the church.

...and how the inexperienced have come to be involved

There were other stirrings of change from within. Right from its inception, the Uniting Church in Australia has affirmed that all members of the church are uniquely gifted for service, and that it is important that representative councils reflect the diversity of the membership of congregations. Deliberate affirmative action had been introduced early in the life of the Uniting Church to address the traditional gender imbalance of very few women representatives on councils and committees of the church. Slowly (O, so slowly!), in some places their contribution was starting to make a difference in the way meetings functioned.

Even more gradually, awareness was growing of the urgency and importance of hearing the voices of youth, of indigenous members and of migrant-ethnic representatives in decision-making councils of the church. The Uniting Church was starting to reflect the increasingly multicultural nature of Australian society, and – like the experience beyond the church – the richness of the resultant tapestry was perceived as both threat and promise. Would the church's structural status quo satisfy the abundant potential that was emerging?

Many of those who were agreeing to be elected to councils of the church from minority sectors were unfamiliar with traditional church meeting procedure. It was often a lonely, frightening, tokenistic path if they did accept appointment. And for long-standing council members, seeing the faces and pronouncing (or more likely mispronouncing!) the unfamiliar names of the increasingly diverse membership of the church was one thing. Hearing the voices (perhaps through interpreters) and benefitting from the insights of those from non-Anglo cultures was another, still a long way from being able to be taken for granted in decision-making throughout the church.

The formal rules of debate make little provision for those whose hesitant, inexperienced voices find it daunting to compete against more eloquent orators. A competent, perceptive chairperson can certainly help, but it needs to be said that at times speakers can be ruthless when they are determined that their perspective will win at whatever cost to others. What's more, unless one is familiar with the intricacies of the amendment process, it is almost impossible for a fresh insight, gleaned during the process of debate, to be included in the wording of the outcome.

The basis of union may affirm "that [Christ] may speak to it [the church] through any of its councils" and that "the task of every council [is] to wait upon God's word, and to obey God's will in the matters allocated to its oversight". But that affirmation was seldom actually tested by pausing in the process to listen for the authoritative voice of the Head of the church. Seeking the wisdom of the Holy Spirit, in trying to discern God's will within the community of those gathered, was rarely invoked through times of silence or prayer once a meeting was underway. The usual opening worship could be quite separate from the substance of the business agenda that followed. Individual piety of members was assumed to have brought the necessary capacity for discernment, through impassioned speeches addressing the issue with integrity – and many a time the church would have affirmed that that was undoubtedly the case in the way matters were resolved.

But often a quiet conversation in the corridors or over a cup of coffee (or perhaps even in the women's restrooms!) disclosed disappointment and disquiet at the way, or the pace at which, a meeting was proceeding. These more intimate exchanges also brought to light the inherent lack of the courage to ask a question or to intervene with a different point of view in what was experienced for many as a hostile environment. These behind-the-scenes corridor conversations, although their importance was probably not appreciated at the time, were actually illustrative of how readily even the most inexperienced people are prepared to engage in sharing insights and developing ideas. It needs simply to be in a medium in which they do not feel threatened, and where they are confident their point of view will be heard and respected.

The concept of community and the building blocks for consensus decision-making were in reality being modelled beyond the council chamber, in spite of adversarial structures and potential power-plays that tended to dominate the formal decision-making of meeting procedure on the other side of the door.

3. Which Way Forward?

After three meetings considering the scope of the work, the task group reported to the assembly standing committee in March 1989 that it felt two complex areas needed to be explored about the way meetings were conducted in councils of the church. Both would need careful consideration before the more pragmatic process could be addressed of formulating specific amendments to the standing orders and rules of debate.

One of these areas was the underlying basis of decision-making for councils of the church, and whether there might be a more appropriate and flexible alternative to the present "parliamentary/argumentative model". The task group had become convinced the church needed to evaluate this basic issue if meetings were to have the freedom to become "creative opportunities for growth rather than avenues of frustration". And then there was the related issue of clarifying the purpose and nature of an assembly meeting in session and the authority its decisions carry throughout the church. The outcome of such an investigation, said the task group, would "influence the process whereby decisions are made and interpreted".

The task group report alerted the assembly standing committee to the possibility that a completely revised set of standing orders might not be ready in time for the sixth assembly in 1991, as had been foreseen originally. But it was recognized that the value of the work being proposed would outweigh any question of expediency in getting amended procedures in place in a rush. So it was agreed the assembly would continue to function under the current standing orders and rules of debate until the full task was completed. Interim reports from the task group to the assembly standing committee would provide avenues for accountability in the meantime, with an expectation of a final submission ready in time for implementation at the seventh assembly in 1994.

How the issues emerged...

Now the task group was free to delve as deeply as they dared into a sound rationale and theological basis for possible different models for decision-making. The potential magnitude of the task they had brought upon themselves was just starting to sink in, along with the daunting realization that this was an unfunded task group. There would be little capacity for researching at first hand the experience of other churches – including those overseas – on a similar quest.

The two areas of investigation proceeded concurrently. The Task Group arranged to meet with officers of the assembly to discuss the different types of purposes for which the assembly in session – and other councils of the church – might need to meet. At the same time, members began to compile material from the experience of other bodies in different meeting procedures, in particular the rationale for decision-making where it was not based on parliamentary procedures.

It was quickly apparent in the discussion with assembly officers that the current standing orders and rules of debate addressed the need for decision-making only, and in a particular style that was not necessarily helpful for all types of personality. As general-purpose guidelines for all meetings of all councils of the church, there were many occasions when these rules were distinctly unhelpful as a framework for proceeding. It was recognized that purposes of meetings vary from assembly (national) to synod (state/territory-based) to presbytery (regional) to church council (local congregation), and that the type of gathering in each forum may be very different for different occasions.

It was acknowledged that a council of the church may meet for many reasons, including inspiration, worship, reflection, information-sharing, information-gathering, affirmation of a group or action, promotion, discussion, fellowship, accountability... and yes, sometimes (but not on every occasion) for deliberately making decisions about issues. The possibility of a variety of models needing to be developed, to suit a range of occasions in the life of the church, was seriously considered in the early stages. And the assembly standing committee had authorized the task group to consider formulating "guidelines to assist all members of a council of the church to participate freely and fairly", rather than simply to reissue conventional rules of debate as the final outcome of the work.

The lack of reflective time in a crowded assembly timetable was another concern raised in the consultation with assembly officers. Over the previous decade, the number of items crammed into a triennial national assembly meeting had increased dramatically, with little expectation of the total agenda being completed before time ran out. More and more unaddressed items were needing to be referred to the assembly standing committee at the end of a national gathering, with the authorization to be handled there on behalf of the assembly. Was it time to be more selective about what was mandated to be decided by the assembly – or indeed by any council of the church?

In spite of these questions being raised at this stage, in reality it would be another few years before the Uniting Church addressed the parallel matter of clarifying and redefining the core functions of each of its councils. The development committee's review of distribution of resources would be presented to the seventh assembly in 1994, the same assembly at which the new procedures would be introduced. It would include a section on church structures that helped clarify the focus of the work of each council of the church, including the assembly.

However, well before that work would be available for adoption by the church, a harder and perhaps more important area of disciplined action needed to be addressed by the task group.

Assembly bodies and commissions were required to bring their reports to the triennial assembly, and these reports overflowed with recommendations which touched on every aspect of their work. (Was there really an uncertainty about what the mandate required that body to accomplish? Or was it a ploy to ensure another five-minute proposer/three-minute seconder opportunity to speak about another aspect of the work of the body?!) It seemed an attitudinal change would be required of assembly members. A mandated body must be allowed to get on with the responsibilities entrusted to it, without needing to present multiple recommendations to legitimize every aspect of its work. Limiting precious meeting time to dealing with important policy issues must become an imperative for business committees.

Clarifying core functions and freeing up the agenda were both essential matters needing simultaneous attention, if changed procedures were to facilitate careful reflection and discernment.

...and how the resources were gathered

There were other hopes noted early by the task group in its deliberations. Some members of the church longed for a less complicated, less obscure language in meetings. ("Previous question" was specifically named as a difficult concept.) The current complex system was prone to different interpretations, tending to favour those with inside knowledge, and at times it could be open to manipulation by "experts". On the other hand, if there were no clear guidelines at all for meeting procedure, the situation could be even more disastrous. It was essential that any alternative model that might be developed actually assisted the participation of ordinary members. They needed to be in possession of full information on a particular issue before being required to vote. The question was raised as to whether a motion, formulated prior to any discussion, was always the most appropriate starting point in seeking a decision on a particular issue. Perhaps the whole background to an issue should be explored, allowing the outcome for the church to become apparent as the discussion developed. Perhaps decisions might sometimes be reached incrementally, as agreement on certain aspects could be relatively easy, while other areas of the issue needed time for further consideration.

And so continued the musings and the brainstorming of creative possibilities within and around meetings of members of the task group, as they sought to address the dilemmas identified. Especially uplifting were the occasions when they met in the Christie-Johnstone home on Philip Island, off

Victoria's southern coastline, in a regular day of annual retreat centred on their task. These were times of energizing focus enriched by beauty and isolation and the warmth of hospitality, and provided opportunity to draw together creatively the separate areas of research which each member had been exploring, and early sections of the draft manual.

Resources were being gathered from the meeting experience of the World Council of Churches, the Christian Conference of Asia, the Australian Council of Churches (now the National Council of Churches in Australia) and the Conference of Churches in Aotearoa New Zealand. There was much to contemplate in the models for meetings used ecumenically, taking into account as they did the diversity of cultural and ecclesial backgrounds of those participating. The theology undergirding decision-making was researched, through a literature search and in personal conversation and correspondence with theologians. The contribution of three hundred years of consensus decision-making through silent discernment in Meetings of the Religious Society of Friends was a valuable resource. So too was the wisdom from our own Uniting Aboriginal and Islander Christian Congress about the traditional indigenous consensus practice in reaching conclusions. Information was filtering through about the awakening interest in North America in different models for meetings, and about the experience of the churches in New Zealand in trying out some new approaches.

In particular, the consensus model adopted by the Methodist Church of Aotearoa New Zealand for their annual conference meeting in 1991 was to be significant.[1] Their process was developed to keep faith with the requirements of New Zealand's Waitangi Treaty between Maori and Great Britain in 1840. The Methodist Church of Aotearoa New Zealand had committed itself to a bi-cultural journey, in which no decisions would be taken by the conference until Maori (indigenes) and Tauiwi (more recent arrivals) were in

1 The information here is based on a report by Rev. Norman McDonald, then general secretary, UCA synod of New South Wales.

agreement. The task group recognized resonating similarities with the earnest desire within Australia to find more mutually enriching ways for Aboriginal and non-Aboriginal members of the church to participate in the councils of the church together. Although the New Zealand consensus model was very different when compared with what was to be the outcome of the Uniting Church's work, we learned much from their concept and practices, and about devising practical details for decision-making sessions in our own model.

The task group was learning from the experience of groups beyond the church as well. Principles used in parent-effectiveness training, in conflict resolution and in legal mediation services were examined, and consideration was given to what enables good small-group dynamics for most effective participation by all.

Surely Christians, meeting as a council of the church, would want to be at least as careful with relationships during discussion and decision-making as secular groups were in using the best of modern management models? Wouldn't they?

4. Why Seek the Common Mind?

What sets the church apart as an organization from secular institutions in determining the outcome of deliberations? This was the basic question the task group set itself to address in fulfilling its obligations to the assembly.

The New Testament records a number of diverse images and examples of how the followers of Jesus are expected to live out their faith in communal life. In Acts 2, the warm, close fellowship of the early Christian groups is expressed in sharing possessions and meals, in caring for the needs of each other, in their joy as they worshipped together and welcomed newcomers into the faith. The way individuals within the community are to act in relation to each other is important to our considerations here. Throughout his letters to churches facing all sorts of problems, Paul speaks frequently of the supportive function each must take in relation to the other, the mutual encouragement that builds faith in one another within the Christian community. But not only do we reach out from strength and security to include and care about the weak and insecure, we also acknowledge our own weakness and vulnerability, and risk acting from that baseline. In fact, as the Philippian church was advised, we are to act in humility, as is the nature of Christ (Phil. 2:5-8).

Why the image of the body is important here...

Being in community is the mutually supportive, empowering and accountable way in which we are able to acknowledge the presence of Jesus Christ in each of his followers. It is Christ himself who alone enables us to achieve and sustain this community, as we share in his life and mission in the world, united in one fellowship of love, service, suffering and joy. It's not only that we find such a model in the New Testament record and throughout the centuries of Christian tradition in the eucharistic community which is the church. When we search deep within our own hearts, we find there a yearning for belonging and acceptance without pretence or fear. As God's forgiving love reaches out to encompass each one just as they are, so we who respond to that grace want to reach out in love to one another – and to all people – as commanded by Jesus.

In helping the young churches understand how to value and respect the unique contribution each member of Christ's community has to offer, Paul uses the image of the body. In his first letter to the church in Corinth, he describes the parts of the human body functioning as an integrated whole. All are dependent on the different capacities each uniquely contributes, yet each needs the others if the whole body with Christ as the Head is to perform to its full potential (12:12-27). In Romans 12:4-5, Paul again presents the body as a model for the church. A similar picture of interdependence and mutuality is found in the first letter of Peter, in the image of the spiritual temple built with living stones with Christ as the cornerstone (2:4-9).

When we look for guidance as to how the New Testament church coped in contentious matters that needed resolution, we find the book of Acts details four specific occasions when communal decision-making is recorded. Within days of the ascension of Jesus, his followers gathered in Jerusalem to appoint a replacement for Judas Iscariot. It was important that the leadership of the Christians continue as a group of twelve apostles, all of whom had been personal witnesses to the resurrection of Jesus (1:14-26). A few chapters later we read of the dispute between Christians who were Greek-speaking Jews and those who were native to Jerusalem, about perceived racial discrimination in the distribution of welfare (6:1-7). Then there was the dramatic confrontation about whether "unclean" gentiles could ever become Christians (11:1-18). And there was the subsequent heated argument about whether gentiles must first become Jews, and thus be required to be circumcized (if they were males) and to obey the law of Moses before they could be baptized as Christians (15:1-33).

We can start to get a feel for how this community of disparate followers of the risen Lord managed (mostly) to remain in fellowship through these contentious issues. We note their reliance on prayer and scripture and on their memories of the teaching of Jesus, in reaching decisions with which all could agree. It seems that, in spite of their differences and the disasters they encountered – or caused – in all their human fallibilities, there was an over-riding sense of purpose in being followers of Jesus, and of being partners with him in his mission in the world. Openness to the guidance of the Holy Spirit and a process for carefully seeking to discern God's will did not come easily when they were faced with huge issues. But we can follow their progress as the letters to the young churches unfold snippets of the history of the early church.

... and why how we make decisions matters

The Uniting Church in Australia proclaims the church is the fellowship of the Holy Spirit. The basis of union declares that

> God in Christ has given to all people in the church the Holy Spirit as a pledge and foretaste of that coming reconciliation and renewal which is the end in view for the whole creation. The church's call is to serve that end: to be a fellowship of reconciliation, a body within which the diverse gifts of its members are used for the building up of the whole, an instrument through which Christ may work and bear witness to himself.

In the Uniting Church, the local congregation is recognized as the basic unit of the community of faith. Councils of the church are appointed from representatives of the membership, people elected because of their gifts for the specific roles asked of them. So in decision-making as the body of Christ, the councils of the church are called to model that fellowship of reconciliation, and to respect the insights of all who have been appointed to particular responsibilities. The church is always searching for the mind of Christ as it seeks to "understand what the will of the Lord is" (Eph. 5:17). The aim is to be able to say with conviction, after consideration of any issue needing resolution, that the outcome "seemed good to the Holy Spirit and to us" (Acts 15:28). Our common commitment is in seeking to discern God's will through the guidance of the Spirit in our deliberations. If it is a genuine commitment, it will be confirmed by the experience of the fruit of the Spirit amongst us as we work – love, joy, peace, patience, kindness, generosity, faithfulness, gentleness and self-control.

The task group concluded that how we make decisions does matter, because the processes we use can shape the pathway for discerning God's will as we model what Christian community is like. Yes, even (or is it especially?) in making decisions on contentious issues, it's important to "be of the same mind, having the same love, being in full accord and of one mind", as the Philippian church was enjoined. It's not going to be easy when we're feeling passionate about a particular point, but we too are urged to "do nothing from selfish ambition or conceit, but in humility [to] regard others as better than yourselves. Let each of you look not to your own interests, but to the interests of others" (Phil. 2:2-4).

In Christian community – and that includes decision-making councils – there's no place for winners and losers on any issue. In the process of seeking to discern God's will for the way forward, we humbly listen for each other's insights. We want to remain open to the unexpected, if we truly yearn for the Spirit's guidance in our work. That's a very different attitude to adopt in a meeting from that of people brought up using adversarial procedures and encouraged from early in their life to develop the win-at-any-cost instinct for success, which apparently is so essential in sport and commerce beyond the church.

Yet that was the challenge in the change that was about to be offered to the church.

5. Whose Contribution Counted?

Gradually the findings of the task group began to crystallize. Tentative sections for a final document were prepared, reconsidered, torn apart and recommissioned. The use of the term "standing orders and rules of debate", for which originally amendments were to be produced, was thought to be a quite unhelpful title for the general direction in which the work was heading. Something more like a "meeting goers manual" (as an early draft was tentatively entitled) appeared likely to emerge, containing significantly more help for all types of church gatherings than simply rules for decision-making procedures.

What the team could now anticipate offering to the church were guidelines with principles for ordered functioning, but with the flexibility to embrace new ways forward as they emerged. Openness to the guidance of the Spirit would mean more intentional focus on worship and the study of the Bible in the course of each meeting. Building community could not just be left to chance but would be specifically described, and would be expected to be intentionally included in the life of each meeting, whatever its size. This was likely to be particularly necessary in large councils which were convened infrequently, and in which it would be rare for there to be continuity of membership.

The task group saw very clearly that the key to the church agreeing to changed procedures would lie in the care with which the underlying principles for the new model were conveyed and understood. A huge mind-shift would be necessary, especially for those who were currently confident that the old procedures were still serving the church well. Already, before the final product had even been put together, there were murmurs of disquiet about the possibility of change. Some were undoubtedly feeling threatened because a familiar power base and forum for flamboyant oratory might be about to be eroded. But there were those who were genuinely uneasy for the sake of the good of the church, concerned that the capacity for in-depth exploration of an issue might be watered down by too ready a willingness to compromise in allowing consensus to be recorded. Or that too ready a focus on agreement within the group itself might disregard implications of the outcome on a wider constituency. The intellectual rigour and stimulation of well-informed debate, it was feared, might be lost forever.

In taking heed of these concerns, the task group determined that the manual would start with sections on why and how we meet in community, carefully identifying the theological foundation for the proposed new model for meetings. It would include resources on best group practice and possibly more than one set of actual decision-making guidelines. Adversarial procedures with majority decision-making were seen by some in the task group (and reluctantly conceded by the others) still to have a place. But the general feeling was that consensus was the goal, in being faithful to their findings about Christians in community working together, with integrity, to seek God's will with the Spirit's guidance.

Reaching consensus in a large meeting

Now this presented a practical dilemma. Breaking an assembly gathering of close to three hundred (and over six hundred for some of the larger synod meetings) into small groups, to explore an issue in depth or to pray for discernment, is a time-consuming logistical manoeuvre that needs careful planning in a complex agenda structure. What's more, waiting for consensus, in both Quaker and traditional Aboriginal indigenous settings, means staying with an issue for as long as it takes for a common mind to be revealed. Whether sitting in silence awaiting discernment in a Meeting of the Religious Society of Friends, or sitting cross-legged in the dust under a eucalyptus tree in outback Australia mulling over a problem, there is no limit placed on how long it takes for a consensus outcome to be reached. But national gatherings of the church in a country the size of Australia are costly exercises in terms of travel and accommodation, let alone in personal sacrifice for participants taking time from work and family responsibilities to participate. It was unthinkable that a planned assembly or synod meeting could be open-ended in duration! So it was decided that the proposal would be based on an assumption that only a few major policy matters would be handled in any assembly or synod meeting.

In the past, an issue for deliberation was presented with the outcome already recommended as the motion for adoption. The case for the presenter's perspective was always the biased starting point. Any alternatives had to be submitted as amendments, and debated in adversarial style in the plenary session. Now the approach was to be different.

Rather than an argued case for one particular, virtually predetermined, outcome being the starting point, a more balanced approach would be necessary for consideration of important issues. It would be essential that presentation of the issue provide members with sufficient information for reaching a decision. It would be important to acknowledge the range of views on the topic that might be held, and to ensure sufficient time for careful attention to each. Breaking into smaller working groups for discussion would be part of the process of deliberation for these few major items. However, occasional buzz groups in plenary sessions, among just two or three people sitting near each other, would be another technique available to the chairperson in every session, ensuring everybody had a chance to share and to hear other insights on whatever was being considered.

In the interests of time, there would need to be a limit on the length of speeches, but not on the number of times any one speaker could seek recognition by the chair to speak. Reaching decisions by these modified, consensus procedures would be the norm, but formal majority procedures would also be detailed in the manual – in a more simplified form than the previous standing orders and rules of debate. While every meeting would include a significant worship and community-building component, the chairperson would use discretion about introducing other opportunities for pausing, praying or even postponing the discussion for a time.

What consensus looks like

In the process of shaping the actual decision-making session, the task group had developed a working model of a flow chart (based on an idea gleaned from a government department) of what were seen to be essential steps in the hitherto unfamiliar consensus procedures. It was thought this visual aid might be a helpful tool for the whole church when it was introduced to the new concept, so work was done on developing the diagrammatic format for inclusion in the manual. The essential elements were identified as:

- Presentation of an issue
- Questions for clarification
- Open discussion of different viewpoints
- Development of possible proposals
- Preparation of a specific proposal
- Discussion of the specific proposal
- Checking for consensus
- Declaration of consensus

If a speaker raised an objection or offered a different idea in the course of the deliberations, at any stage it would be possible to return to an earlier point in the flow of the meeting, exploring the new thought until an outcome could be reached. The absence of formal motions and amendments would immediately free up the flow of discussion, and open the way for new concepts to be discovered and woven into the deliberations.

Consensus was described as a process by which the common mind of the meeting was sought. This could be unanimous, or by agreement where a small minority agreed to set aside their objections so the council could proceed to determine the matter. (After six years of use in the church, when the procedures were reviewed "consensus" and "agreement" would be separated and recognized as two distinct outcomes in the way a decision was reached.)

Where a meeting remained polarized, steps were included to give opportunity for the council to consider whether a decision needed to be taken immediately, or whether the matter might be referred elsewhere for further consideration or more work. If the council agreed the matter should be finalized forthwith and it was clear that consensus would not be achieved, a process to enable moving into formal majority procedures would be activated and the matter determined by majority vote.

The value of cards and colour

It was the casual introduction of a somewhat unlikely idea in the course of the task group's work that surprisingly was to become the "trade-mark" symbol of the Uniting Church's consensus procedures. One of the group members happened to mention, almost as an aside, that he had experienced the use of indicator cards as he participated in meetings for his secular employment body. Different colours had signified "for" or "against", and they had been waved at any stage during a speech, in support of or with antagonism for the views being expressed. They had also been used as voting cards.

The use of cards sparked a lively discussion amongst task group members. What gradually caught their imagination was using a visual means of identifying a growing consensus during the course of a discussion. Excitement started to mount, that Sunday afternoon in the suburban manse living room where the task group was meeting, as different possibilities were casually tossed back and forth. At the time, banter about the use of coloured cards felt like a little light relief in the midst of other more serious work still to be accomplished. After all, a deadline was threateningly close.

Yet this seemingly trivial interlude became the breeding ground of what would be recognized (erroneously, as it happens!) as the hallmark of consensus procedures, throughout the Uniting Church in Australia and for observers well beyond our church.

What emerged was the use of the now very familiar orange and blue indicator cards, issued to voting members of a particular council. An added advantage (only to become apparent later) was that use of the cards, by authorized members of the council only, would cut down on the need to have a clearly defined "bar of the house" or physical dividing line between those entitled to vote and those not. Blue and orange were not randomly chosen (and they had not been the colours of the prototypes used in the work-place meeting from which the concept developed). They were selected after careful thought because they are distinguishable as separate colours by those who are colour-blind. The perhaps more obvious traffic-light equivalents of red for stopping – or opposition – and green for moving on – or support – would have made it impossible for some to identify the separate cards. However, even those who carry a colour-differentiation deficiency in vision can distinguish between blue and orange. And with orange as a warm colour and blue as a cool one, there's immediately an easy way of remembering which card indicates warmth towards a speaker's point, or coolness towards the idea being expressed.

The novelty of the cards provided a quick and obvious way to start the process of introducing the new procedures. Being issued with cards signified immediately to all members of a council that this was going to be a very different approach. And there was the intriguing factor of hands-on involvement right from the start, emphasizing as it did one of the basic premises of the new approach – that every member's point of view is important and valued. Very quickly, it brought to light the need for more focused concentration by all throughout council proceedings, as old habits of sitting passively and silently (or even dozing!) through a meeting were no longer possible. When members of a council were asked to show their response to something that had just been said, each had to be able to express an opinion by holding up one card or the other!

And the birth came to pass

Initial trials of the embryo procedures took place in a number of presbytery (regional council) meetings in and around Melbourne, Victoria, where the task group was based. The team showed deep appreciation of the earnestness with which participants in meetings submitted to being the guinea pigs, enabling queries to be addressed and rough edges to be smoothed before the final document was completed.

In September 1992 the draft manual was received by the assembly standing committee and released for comment and more formal trial use in the church. Briefing sessions for potential leaders of the trials, including all synod secretaries, were held in Sydney, New South Wales, and Melbourne, Victoria (the capital cities of the two most populous states). Trials in presbyteries and church councils in various parts of the country occurred from April to July 1993, and then in meetings of the synods of Tasmania and Western Australia in October of that year. Comments from various parts of the church led to further minor amendment, before the assembly standing committee received the final version in March 1994.

The assembly standing committee endorsed the proposal of the business committee for *A Manual for Meetings in the Uniting Church* to be used at the seventh assembly in July 1994. The document was sent to all members of that assembly meeting well ahead of time, to ensure opportunity for possible use in local church councils beforehand and for absorbing the rationale and detail of the changes about to be experienced in the conduct of the assembly.

At the commencement of the seventh assembly in Sydney in July 1994, members of the task group engagingly introduced the new procedures in the first session through explanation, illustration and role-play. The church was helped in a smooth change-over from old to new by those who happened to be in office at the time. Both the incoming president (the author), who chaired the assembly meeting, as well as the then general secretary (Gregor Henderson) had been privileged to join with the task group in the latter half of its working life. Along with members of the business committee, their familiarity with the new guidelines, and more importantly their passionate conviction about the theological basis and the appropriateness of the change, enabled a relaxed approach to some of the stickier moments that inevitably had to be faced.

Midwifing the birth of changed procedures in the church required some on-the-spot chairing decisions about aspects that could not have been foreseen. But with these consensus procedures, there is always reassurance in the awareness that the meeting will determine what it will. So when there was doubt about how to proceed, a way forward was put to the meeting for approval (by consensus, of course!). Experimenting with the flexible options of the guidelines became an exciting way of exploring the scope of the new procedures throughout the sessions of the assembly week.

Members of that seventh assembly in 1994 are to be commended for the candour and enthusiasm with which they entered into the unfamiliar consensus processes, paving the way adventurously yet graciously for their subsequent introduction throughout the rest of the church.

6. What Happened?

There's no doubt this was a momentous change in the life of the Uniting Church. Yet until the seventh assembly actually resolved to adopt the new procedures in its first business session, the six years of concentrated work and wisdom of the task group still hung in the balance.

Constitutionally, amending the current standing orders and rules of debate could only be done by the assembly itself in respect of its own business, and there was a very real possibility that the assembly, once it was convened, would decline to introduce the new procedures. So the business committee had been required to plan the agenda for either contingency, and many a breath was bated until the decision to proceed was taken. The moment the resolution was approved, rejoicing was palpable. That first collective sigh of relief by task group members, the business committee and the officers of the assembly must have fluttered agenda papers in the highest tier of seats in the auditorium of the University of New South Wales, in which we were meeting!

The decision is recorded in these words:

> The Assembly resolved to adopt the procedures of *A Manual for Meetings in the Uniting Church* for the business of the seventh assembly... including the use of working groups and voting cards.

And at the end of the assembly week, with even more enthusiasm it was resolved

> to request the standing committee to revise *A Manual for Meetings in the Uniting Church* following evaluation of its use at this assembly and to commend *A Manual for Meetings in the Uniting Church*, after revision, for use by the councils of the church in place of the current standing orders.

Participants in the 1994 assembly had received copies of the manual in their working papers well before the assembly started. But it had been an extraordinary hope that they would immediately be able to absorb the details, let alone readily accept a new way of conducting business in a week-long national gathering, where significant decisions awaited their consideration.

What happened at the assembly...

There were big issues to be addressed at that seventh assembly – matters of world and national significance, of reconciliation and justice, and of internal ordering and functioning. Matters to do with ministry always activate the big guns when there's a hint of change to the status quo. And proposals to be addressed by this assembly meeting had much to do with ministry changes. They included:

- recognition of two distinct ordinations, one for ministry of the word and one for deacon, and the mutuality and equality of both; discussion on this was spiced up by a motion from the assembly doctrine commission, which sought to rescind the previous assembly's decision to ordain deacons;
- the question of whether ministers who refuse to baptize infants could continue to have a place within the Uniting Church;
- the establishment of community ministry as a new lay specified ministry;
- a proposal to set up a task group to review ministerial education;
- approval of a whole new section of the regulations on dealing with complaints of sexual abuse by ministers.

The scene was set for a fascinating week's work – dynamic, demanding and potentially polarizing. The major issues were each presented in a plenary session, then adjourned for working groups to explore in some depth, or to reflect quietly and pray about, before returning to a deliberation and decision session.

For some participating, particularly those more timid or unaccustomed to the use of complex procedural ploys, the fresh approach of the new procedures was engaged with eagerness and relief. But there was also an attitude of suspicion and resentment on the part of a few. For some experienced orators, their confidence in the use of the old system had at times resulted in the manipulation of a meeting to ensure that their point of view predominated. At this assembly, the participation of people with a particular perspective was certainly still passionate. However, the new procedures succeeded in keeping the focus on continually seeking to discern the best way forward for the church, notwithstanding anyone's preferred position.

At the end of the assembly week, it was gratifying to hear one old warrior of the previous parliamentary procedures say, "I was so sure this new model for meetings wouldn't work, that valid debate would be stifled. Now I'd just like to say – if we hadn't been using the new consensus procedures for those ministry matters, we'd be walking away from here as a divided church today. I think you've made the right move!"

One group in the life of the assembly who were particularly challenged by consensus decision-making were those who record the minutes. Because of the flexibility in the use of the procedures, the original wording of a proposal under discussion can be drastically different by the time a consensus decision is ready to be recorded. We were grateful for the availability of data projection, so that what was being typed continually by the recorders was available for displaying at any time. This ensured that members of the assembly were confident of the words on which consensus was being sought before a matter was finalized.

Adding to the mix throughout the week, for the first time this seventh assembly incorporated a visitors programme, a programme for children, and guests from other faiths as well as ecumenical representatives. There was opportunity,amidst the illuminating and instructive options arranged for each of these groups, for them to sit in on business sessions from time to time and observe at first hand what the changed procedures looked like in action. And youth representatives, while fully participating elected members of the assembly, had gathered in pre-assembly sessions to be briefed on the agenda issues: during that time they had eagerly embraced the new consensus procedures.

So right from its introduction, the concept of consensus was reaching a far wider membership of the church – and beyond – than we had anticipated, which gave a running start to the broader dissemination to follow.

... and what happened later in the synods and councils

The church was well served by those who had been present at the seventh assembly (both members and observers), in the way they assisted in the subsequent introduction of the new procedures in synods, presbyteries and church council meetings around the country. Although the assembly had commended the use of the new procedures to replace the standing orders and rules of debate throughout the church, it was still a constitutional prerogative of each council to determine which procedures they would use. Certainly all synods (the seven state/territory based councils) and most presbyteries (the 52 regional councils) were keen to be at the forefront of the change throughout the church. Officers of all those councils had been members of the seventh assembly, whereas not every congregation (from which church councils are elected) would have had a member with first-hand experience to help demythologize what the change was all about.

The process of educating the church about *A Manual for Meetings in the Uniting Church in Australia* was the next big undertaking in the Uniting Church's journey with consensus procedures. The slightly amended version (in light of experience in the 1994 assembly meeting) was published early in 1995. Since then, it – or its revision – has been included every time the constitution and regulations of the Uniting Church in Australia have been published.

Consensus procedures demand much of the person chairing the meeting. It's a very different role from that in formal majority procedures, for which the chairperson is expected to remain detached from the substance of the debate and largely just direct the traffic according to the rules. With consensus procedures, chairpersons carry a range of demanding responsibilities:

- remaining constantly alert for evidence of the Spirit's guidance through the contributions of members;
- encouraging trust and integrity in contributions;
- ensuring care and support for those whose honesty may leave them vulnerable;

- pausing for prayer or silent reflection as appropriate;
- specifically inviting comment from those uneasy with the majority viewpoint;
- listening for (or at times suggesting) creative modifications of a proposal which will pick up insights expressed by different members;
- and summarizing the discussion to assist in focusing where the mind of the meeting is heading.

Moderators of each synod (who chair the synod meetings) gathered in Sydney for a time of prayer and reflection with the president soon after the 1994 assembly meeting. We took that opportunity specifically to work through a practical session on using consensus procedures. And in the annual face-to-face gathering of moderators with the president for the three years following, we continued to learn from each other's experience in the use of consensus procedures. Regrettably, equipping presbytery chairpersons was not such an intentional or thorough an exercise, although a number of presbyteries sought specific training for their members and officers, to ensure they achieved the best possible outcome from the new model for meetings they were adopting.

The church press in every synod helpfully took up the story with enthusiasm. Soon members of the Uniting Church from one end of the country to the other could not help but be aware that something different was happening in councils of the church, even if they were not personally directly involved. But public awareness is not the same as every church member understanding the process thoroughly, and engaging in it locally.

The assembly standing committee was very anxious that the momentum and enthusiasm evident in the 1994 assembly meeting should not be lost. A very helpful leaflet had been prepared in 1993 by Ann Siddall, from the Centre for Christian Spirituality in the UCA synod of South Australia. This was intended to complement the introduction of the new procedures, and offered excellent suggestions and resources for worship and community-building in meetings, focusing specifically on spiritual discernment. An educational kit for introducing the manual was prepared by Marelle Harisun, then general secretary of the synod of South Australia. This incorporated an action-reflection process for understanding the principles, and role-plays to enliven the theory with practical relevance. The kit was tested in several settings, and has continued to be used informally from time to time, but unfortunately has never been officially adopted or used widely. Ongoing equipping of all church members in effective use of consensus procedures is still sadly deficient in the Australian experience.

Over the three years after the seventh assembly, synods in particular continued to develop the processes to suit the needs of large gatherings. The use of small working groups is an essential key to full participation when hundreds are meeting in council, and efficient and rapid feedback from these groups is most important. The synods' experience was germane to developing the concept of the facilitation group (which the first edition of *A Manual for Meetings in the Uniting Church in Australia* mentions briefly only in its appendix) into a valued part of the process.

Moving forward to the eighth assembly...

The facilitation group comprises a small number of people with a broad understanding of the church and the issues being faced, people with good listening, analytical and negotiating skills, and with the capacity to draw contributions together into carefully worded proposals for consideration by a council. Their role is:

- to coordinate responses from small-group work;
- to ensure that all insights are considered in working towards consensus about the way forward for any issue; and
- to ensure that reworded proposals coming before the council have been negotiated with the original proposers and all small-group leaders.

The church has been blessed time and again by the wisdom and sensitivity of those serving on facilitation groups in this way, and we have rejoiced in the fruits of their endeavours in consensus outcomes on some difficult issues.

People's growing confidence in chairpersons and business committees about the use of the procedures during the years 1994 to 2000 saw other techniques develop. One that has been particularly helpful in contentious matters is clarifying the fundamental issues underlying diverse opinions on an issue. It may be that, by breaking a complex topic down into more basic fragments, a meeting can be helped to make progress one step at a time. Often there is much that can be affirmed with confidence out of our one allegiance to Jesus Christ; then sticking points can be clarified more readily, and considered in the context of that recognition of common ground.

This was certainly true during the eighth assembly when it convened in Perth, Western Australia, in 1997. Perth considered the polarizing issue of homosexual leadership with much agony and with demarcation lines apparently drawn well before the assembly meeting was actually convened. Consensus procedures enabled us to listen to each other and to the voice of the Spirit, as moving testimonies were offered in the plenary deliberation sessions, and small groups prayed together for discernment. In the end there was unanimity. We reached consensus that the church could affirm a number of basic principles about sexuality and human relationships. And there was also consensus that the church would be prepared to live with divergent points of view about other issues to do with sexuality, where no single directive could be offered to the church as God's discerned will for the way forward at that time. That was by no means the end of polarizing opinions within the church about homosexual leadership – the debate continues to this day! But we did manage in that 1997 assembly to reach consensus about some fundamental affirmations to do with sexuality.

... and the status quo elsewhere

While in assembly and synod councils the new procedures were being used with increasing confidence, the same could not be said universally for presbyteries (regional councils) and church councils (in congregations). Some, it is true, were quickly able to make the transition and experience the liberating relief that openness to the guidance of the Spirit in a meeting can bring. Where that occurred locally, it was largely due to the commitment of individuals who were familiar with the consensus model from wider involvement in the life of the church. But other councils chose to continue to function as they always had, dealing with motions and amendments, engaging in adversarial speeches for and against, and voting for a simple majority to decide issues.

Elected officers of local church councils do not necessarily remain in office for a lengthy term, so there could be little certainty of a growing familiarity with the different model for meetings. For some, it was almost as if the hot topic of consensus had been merely a momentary blip on the wider screen, but when faced with the local reality of making decisions, a council automatically reverted to what had been the familiar (and the only) way in the past. In fact, when challenged on using what were by this stage outdated procedures, it was common for recalcitrant chairpersons just to laugh it off dismissively, assuming the challenger could not seriously be suggesting that the novel new "soft" approach should really be used for serious business.

It was clearly time for a more formal assessment of how widely the consensus procedures had been accepted by the Uniting Church as a whole.

7. Where Did We Need to Improve?

After six years of using the consensus model for meetings (1994-2000), a review of the changed procedures was undertaken. Assessing the positive outcomes for the church, as well as taking heed of difficulties encountered, would determine what learnings we might helpfully incorporate into a revision of *A Manual for Meetings in the Uniting Church in Australia*.

The assembly standing committee appointed a small review group (chaired by the author), who set about the task by inviting comment from the church in general. We also personally approached a wide selection of those who had used the procedures in very diverse situations over that six-year period. The contributions and feedback produced some penetrating comment about the theory in the manual, as well as about the practice of the procedures.

A more deliberately worshipful atmosphere

But the main message to come through in the review was that there was overwhelmingly positive support for the introduction of the manual, and for continuing the consensus model for meetings. A strong feeling was expressed in many quarters that the ethos in councils of the Uniting Church was changing, attributable, it was averred, in no small part to the use of the new procedures for meetings. Respondents spoke of an improved sense of community and mutual accountability. The comment was made that the church had been enriched by greater patient openness to hearing what the Spirit is saying through its councils.

An expectation had been built into the guidelines that every meeting would set aside at least twenty percent of its time for worship and community-building, and use opportunities to pause for reflection and prayer as appropriate while an issue was being considered. As well as these enriching opportunities, it was found that listening for the guidance of the Spirit had also been enhanced through valuing more respectfully the insights of all who carry responsibilities as council members. Although the "worshipful work" concept, being developed in North America by Charles Olsen and others[1] around this same period, was not named as such in our procedures, in many councils a more deliberately worshipful atmosphere was now noted as the norm in business meetings.

It was clear in reviewing the meeting experience of the church since 1994 that, as had been anticipated, among those who had benefitted significantly from the changed procedures were the quieter voices, so often overlooked in the past. These included laywomen and young people, whose review comments noted that respecting each other's contribution and ending up in agreement is the natural way of informal conversations, often leading to an agreed course of action without dissension in daily life. Newcomers to council membership, indigenous members, and those for whom English was not their first language spoke appreciatively of the intentional community-building aspect, finding a growing confidence in trusting others when interacting within small-group settings.

However, the matter was also raised of respecting the first-language preference of those for whom the use of English is difficult for communicating ideas. The manual was published only in English. Yet there are migrant-ethnic and indigenous congregations of the Uniting Church in Australia worshipping week by week in any one of up to forty other languages, including a number of Aboriginal tribal languages. Communication of the new procedures had been sadly deficient for all these members of the church.

Some respondents commented on their satisfaction that fewer issues, but more carefully prioritized ones, are now considered in depth in a meeting with a limited timespan. As intended, the work in assembly and synod meetings is more focused and more deliberately confined to dealing with the core responsibilities of that body. And greater ownership of decisions is an important result of emphasizing the participation of every member of a council of the church in seeking to

---

1 Danny E. Morris and Charles M. Olsen, *Discerning God's Will Together*, Bethesda MD, Alban Institute, 1997.

discern God's will for the church. Once the meeting is over, all participating may now be expected to be advocates for the outcome.

Experienced moderators are essential

Of course there were criticisms. Many of the negative reactions related to inappropriate handling of procedures by inexperienced chairpersons. A few sought a clearer theological statement of the basis for the model, and we were helped here by the contribution of more than one theologian. Some provided suggestions for modifications to the guidelines to address particular concerns.

It came as no surprise to hear that there is need for more rigorous, intentional, ongoing training of those with chairing responsibilities. Some councils had made no attempt to make the change in procedures or, having agreed to do so, had taken no steps to ensure the chairperson was adequately equipped for the role. There had been a naïve assumption on the part of the assembly standing committee that, in handing over office from old to new chairpersons in presbyteries and church councils, something of the experience and familiarity with the new procedures would have been transmitted. However, this was often not the case. Inconsistency and uncertainty in chairing skills can quickly destabilize a council's confidence in both chairperson and procedures, and poor decisions and dissatisfaction among participants are likely to be the outcome.

We discovered in some places a bizarre hybrid of old and new practices, bearing little resemblance to the intended consensus model or to the previous formal majority procedures! We became aware of presbyteries claiming to have introduced the new procedures, and yet the only change had been to issue members with coloured indicator cards to use in voting. Voting cards – and no other change – meant consensus in that unfortunately limited understanding! Even where genuine attempts had been made to follow the guidelines faithfully, inexperienced chairpersons still at times found themselves trapped in an apparent impasse. It does take time and experience with the processes to be able to persevere with confidence through to a consensus outcome on difficult issues.

Another concern was that radical debate was being muffled, where the procedures were not being handled carefully enough. A good chairperson would not allow this to happen, but it had occurred supposedly in the interests of time and out of a short-sighted anxiety to reach a harmonious conclusion. The resultant "lowest common denominator" outcome had brought about feelings of disquiet and dissatisfaction with the process. It is important to remember that the last uneasy voice expressing disquiet against majority opinion might actually be channelling the quiet guidance of the Spirit. Care must be taken to take every contribution seriously. Seeking to discern the will of God requires a thorough exploration of the issue, before the deliberations are drawn together into a consensus decision about the best way forward for the church – not only locally, but in the broader ecumenical and international arenas also.

These concerns pointed to one of the sections in the manual that needed sharpening as a result of the review. It is essential right at the start in the presentation session that all aspects of an issue are aired fully. Differing points of view must be thoroughly researched and competently presented. Consensus is not intended to mean compromise, but an informed and genuine working through with integrity and vigour to discover a way forward on which all can agree, taking all points of view into consideration.

The review group discovered that some councils and chairpersons were using the provision in the manual for moving from consensus mode into formal procedures too readily. For some it's as if, after a token attempt to give consensus a try, it's simpler to revert to a majority vote and get the issue finalized. This irregularity also brought to light the lack of awareness of the simplified formal majority procedures contained in the manual. But it seems that for many people the mystery of the old procedures still continues to be an insurmountable barrier to full participation in the meeting life of the church. That feeling of alienation from participation is certainly not helped by councils of the church that persist in using the old model.

As a consequence of these comments, we clarified the steps in the consensus process and revised the flow chart accordingly. Formal majority procedures were pared back to essentials, both in simpler language and in fewer steps to follow. We assumed that from now on they would be used less and less – only on the rare occasions when consensus was not able to finalize a decision. A flow chart for formal majority procedures was also included in the revised manual, so that those more familiar by this stage with the consensus model would not be disadvantaged when the alternative procedures did need to be used.

It was found necessary to include a comment in the revised manual about the place of proxy and absentee votes. Under consensus procedures these can never be permissible, as it is in community together that the way forward is discerned progressively. No predetermined position, or expectation that a member will stand firm for a particular factional point of view, is compatible with the fundamental principle of openness to the Spirit's guidance.

Techniques for chairpersons

The review group realized that chairpersons needed to be aware of more techniques to avoid the pressure to move too quickly into formal majority procedures in order to resolve an apparently stalemated situation. Some of those techniques include:

- encouraging the meeting specifically to explore what might be a way forward that takes into account the insights already offered: challenging members to think beyond their preferred option, to the broader picture developing, can release some really creative possibilities;
- summarizing the discussion to the point reached, and crystallizing what the core of the real issue is, beyond the words that are currently being debated;

- redefining the basic question needing resolution, and perhaps reaching consensus on small steps rather than the entire matter as it has been presented;
- breaking for buzz groups for a few minutes, just where people are sitting: this can sometimes be the safety valve that unlocks the jam;
- pausing for prayer, seeking guidance about the way forward as a whole council;
- adjourning discussion for a tea break – sometimes this can be all that's needed, as the solution may emerge while members mingle and muse informally;
- encouraging the council to agree, by consensus, that the matter be deferred for further consideration;
- encouraging the council to agree, by consensus, to refer the matter to another group to resolve;
- encouraging the council to agree, by consensus, to accept that Christians may hold a range of views on this matter, with equal integrity.

The constraints of limited time was another problem identified, in spite of the task group's orginal attempts to get the church to address ways to avoid this. A crowded agenda does not encourage careful participatory discernment. Feedback from small-group work is often time-consuming in large councils, and business committees must always give careful thought to ways of streamlining this essential aspect. This will include consideration of the best way of collating small-group contributions, to resource the plenary for making a decision about the issue. A more complete description of the role of the facilitation group was consequently included in the revised manual.

As a result of the review group's findings, some practical changes were introduced as the text was simplified and the processes were streamlined in the revised manual. For instance, it was agreed it was time to standardize the language used, and to avoid the use of terms that evoked memories of another model for meetings. Hence consensus procedures now speak of "proposal" rather than "motion", "variation" rather than "amendment", "proposer" instead of "mover". (But the small section on formal majority as an available procedural option does retain the old terms more familiar in that setting.)

The use of the indicator cards

Even the way indicator cards are used has seen some development. At the end of any speech, a member is encouraged to show a card to indicate a response to what has just been said, thus assisting the person chairing to ascertain how many others in the council concur with the sentiments just expressed. Rather than flamboyant waving of cards (which may be quite confrontational and polarizing), the revised explanation of their use now invites members to hold a card discreetly at chest level, so the chairperson can inform the council of the response to the last speech more courteously.

There had been a tendency to use the blue card (showing opposition or coolness) as a tool for seeking further opportunity to speak. In the process of testing for consensus when the council is almost of one mind, the one or two still unable to support the way forward would show blue cards when all are asked to indicate their opinion. People holding minority opinions are usually then asked if they want to speak, to help the meeting understand why they are unable to support what most of the others are finding helpful at this stage. Some councils found that this was used as a means to be heard again, even if there was in fact no opposition to the way forward being proposed.

Educating the church to limit its use of cards to expressions of opinion has not been an easy process! Members wishing to speak are now encouraged not to wave a card of one colour or another, but to stand, or line up at a microphone, or indicate it to the chairperson in some other way. (One synod has actually introduced the use of a third card, neutral in colour, to be used to indicate a desire to speak. The rationale is that it allows a more even-handed contribution without necessarily having to declare support or opposition before speaking.)

Another way of using the cards was reported as particularly helpful to the flow of a meeting. When a council member feels debate is being extended unduly, or a speech is too long or becoming repetitive, it is possible to signify it is time to move on by holding both cards crossed at chest level. The chairperson is able to see this discreet hint from one or more members, and take steps to move on without having to hear disruptive points of order before taking action.

A shift of attitude

The biggest challenge brought to light in reviewing the introduction of consensus procedures was the attitudinal shift still needed for some members of the church. Expecting one point of view on a particular issue will "win" assumes a triumph over those who obviously must "lose". Yet unity and humility are key characteristics of the body of Christ. Our desire to seek God's will as a community will surely be stronger than our personal passion to see a particular position prevail. There can be no winners or losers. All who participate rejoice when the agreed outcome takes us forward as a church to risk following the way of Jesus, even though it may be a challenging way.

Openness to hearing the guidance of the Spirit through other voices, especially those with ideas opposed to one's own, can actually transform the whole ambience of a meeting. All meetings can be occasions for eager anticipation, awaiting what will be revealed as the way forward on any issue. It may be totally different from any of the preconceived outcomes members may have brought to the meeting initially.

As a result of the review process, the review group was able to streamline the guidelines and simplify the text in the manual. The ninth assembly readily approved the amendments to the manual in 2000, and agreed to make provision in the regulations for the revised version, *A Manual for Meetings 2000,* to be the standard for meeting procedures throughout the church. These would now be the norm for all councils of the church – national, state, regional and local.

The visionary course laid out so valiantly by the original task group on standing orders in 1988 was now the agreed pathway of promise into the future. The potential for meetings to be "creative opportunities for growth", as had been the task group's vision six years earlier, now had the framework to become a reality. It would be the church's responsibility to ensure it was used to full effect!

8. What's Essential in Introducing Consensus?

The consensus procedures developed for the Uniting Church in Australia are guidelines rather than rules. As such, we have found them to be flexible enough for use at a major national assembly as much as for a local church council or for a sub-committee of just a few people.

The principles that are universal, whatever the context, are summarized in this chapter under four headings, as follows.

Theological basis

- conviction that God has a way forward for the church
- reliance on the guidance of the Holy Spirit in seeking to discern that way
- recognition that all are gifted by God, and that we need each other to function effectively in the church
- respect for each member's contribution
- openness to hearing the voice of the Spirit through the contribution of those with whom I disagree as much as through those who agree with me
- willingness to risk an unexpected outcome, if that is the meeting's discernment

The Uniting Church in Australia is a non-hierarchical Christian church, arising from the Reformed and Evangelical traditions of Protestantism. It is a national church, governed through a system of inter-related councils (national assembly, state synods, regional presbyteries and local church councils). Each of these councils has specific areas of responsibility, all of them directly or indirectly resulting in equipping the congregation, as described in the basis of union, to be the "embodiment in one place of the one holy catholic and apostolic church of Jesus Christ, worshipping, witnessing and serving as a fellowship of the Spirit in Christ".

Not every denomination is structured or functions in this manner. The theological basis summarized here is drawn from the Uniting Church's conviction that "Christ alone is supreme in his church, and that he may speak to it through any of its councils. It is the task of every council to wait upon

God's word, and to obey God's will in the matters allocated to its oversight."

Unless members of a council of the church are committed to the biblical concepts of community and mutuality, no amount of tinkering with amendment to by-laws will bring about change. If "I want to win at any cost to others" remains in the heart of participants, no procedures can be immune from subversive manipulation and divisive outcome.

Functional aspects

- community-building
- opportunity for all to contribute
- fair exploration of the range of perspectives surrounding an issue
- agenda design

Community-building starts with the acknowledgment of our common allegiance to the lordship of Christ. Community begins as we join in worship together and affirm our faith and our commitment to follow in the way of Jesus. Other opportunities for developing community occur as we sing together, laugh together, celebrate cultural diversity and difference together, eat together. Numbers don't signify when we engage in these communal interactions for a common purpose. Small or large, we do them together.

But the way trust develops in a gathering **is** dependent on the numbers involved. Where many hundreds meet, it is necessary to break into small groups to ensure opportunity for personal sharing, mutual accountability, and caring awareness of each other's situation. The support of a constant small group throughout a week of meetings can provide a secure home base, a place where reflecting, debriefing, praying, weeping, laughing... can be entered into with safety, and out of which can emerge a greater strength and confidence to participate in the larger forum.

When a small committee meeting consists of perhaps ten people commissioned with a specific task, community-building does not need to be so structured. Opportunity can be given at the start of the meeting for each one to indicate what has been significant in their lives in the past week, for instance. Such a simple brief interaction can be enough to break down isolating barriers, even if group members know each other well in the first place.

For large gatherings, the venue must be selected and the agenda arranged with care, so that breaking for small-group work is not an awkward intrusion into the day's movements. Time spent in building community is never wasted in a meeting's agenda. To gather and commence business instantaneously sets the scene for awkwardness and mistrust. What may seem like time-wasting personal interactions can in fact build a bedrock of mutuality and growing trust, on which subsequent deliberations will flow more smoothly.

The Uniting Church's *Manual for Meetings 2000* recommends twenty percent of total time be set aside intentionally for this community-building, including worship. The benefits in the way members of councils of the church are equipped and the meeting proceeds will more than compensate for this time being unavailable for business.

In small meetings, a chairperson may need to be on the alert for the quiet one who needs encouragement to express a view, or for the talkative one who is full of ideas needing to be shared! Even in a meeting of only eight or ten members, it may be wise occasionally to suggest breaking into buzz groups of three or four, to give different people the chance to contribute. For a larger council, the business committee will need to incorporate into the timetable more structured small-group work, for considering issues in depth and for praying for discernment.

When presentation of an issue covers the broad spectrum of views known to be held with integrity by Christians, all members are more likely to relax in the assurance that their particular point of view is already being taken seriously. The ensuing discussion is less likely to be fuelled by resentment and defensive volatility, and can focus on genuinely debating the issues. The scene is better set for an open, objective consideration of where the way forward lies. Agreement by the meeting to listen to speakers without interjection or applause is a courtesy that can encourage a respectful, non-threatening hearing of views, particularly for very contentious issues. It can be agreed that showing indicator cards at the end of a speech (or otherwise indicating a response at the invitation of the chairperson) should be the only way feelings are registered.

For each major issue on the agenda of a council meeting that lasts for several days, it will be important to schedule the presentation session early on. This will allow time for small-group discussion on them before returning to the whole council for further deliberation and then decision at a later stage. The Uniting Church in Australia has found the first part of a week-long agenda can be carefully detailed prior to the meeting actually convening, ensuring that major issues are presented in depth prior to time for small-group work on them. But the agenda for the last days of the meeting needs to remain fairly flexible until it is clear which of the early deliberations will require more time for development.

Chairperson's role

- confidence in the process, which breeds confidence in the council members' participation
- expectation that the way forward will emerge
- alertness to an insight that could be developed further
- capacity to define the underlying issues on which consensus is really necessary
- discernment time – pausing for prayer and silent reflection as part of any decision-making
- calling for response at the end of a speech, and reflecting it back to the meeting
- knowing how to check for consensus, and what to do when it's not yet reached

Careful preparation of those who will be called upon to chair sessions is essential. The Uniting Church in Australia has not carried this principle through as carefully as it should have, as office-bearers have changed over the years. There is no doubt that the model stands or falls on the skill with which the person chairing encourages the meeting to keep searching for the way forward, a way that takes into account the insights expressed by participants. A chairperson needs to keep alert to the scope of the discussion, and be ready to offer a summary of what is being said to help focus the direction.

Being relaxed about the outcome helps. Being confident in the guidance of the Spirit is essential. Being aware of some of the practical options available is wise.

- *A Manual for Meetings 2000* suggests wording for questions to assist a chairperson in checking for consensus. It's quite helpful to have the wording nearby during a session!
- Often small changes can be finalized by consensus as the discussion proceeds, or underlying fundamentals affirmed where superficial diversity remains.
- It's important to recognize that consensus may be reached when all are *opposed* to a particular proposal as much as when all are in *favour*; and that the council can decide by consensus that the matter be postponed pending further work. There is never only one outcome possible, so all need to remain alert to creative discernment.
- Where it seems impossible for consensus to be achieved, the chairperson can guide the meeting in one of a number of ways:
  – The few unable to agree with the majority opinion may be able to acknowledge they have been fairly heard, and that they are prepared to live with the outcome discerned by the majority. The minutes then can record agreement (rather than consensus) to approve the proposal.
  – There may be a more basic question to be addressed than the proposal as it stands. The chairperson may be able to focus the issue to what *can* be affirmed by all. Often the council then decides by consensus to defer the rest of the issues to a later session, or for further work to be done; or agree there is a diversity of positions that Christians may take with equal integrity.
  – On rare occasions, there will be some urgency to achieve a definitive outcome immediately. The coun-

cil should be invited to consider objectively whether it is essential to finalize it at that session; if so, the procedures then allow for a mechanism to revert to formal majority procedures to decide the issue.

Practical points

- selection of venue
- visual and auditory aids
- language interpreters
- keeping minutes
- preparation of those with specific responsibilities

Because small-group work is integral to the effective participation of all council members, for a large gathering the logistics of relocating hundreds of people quickly and smoothly is an important consideration. The venue needs to be selected with space sufficient for the entire council, whatever its size, to meet in table groups of no more than ten people each throughout plenary sessions. This enables a quick and easy way to pause for prayer or discussion in a small group, without having to lose time relocating from the plenary hall. It is generally also wise to have ready access to enough other sites for groups to reconvene at specific times for intentional small-group work. Feedback from these working groups will need to be collated, perhaps by a specifically designated facilitation group, so the group sites should not be too widely scattered. For the Uniting Church in Australia, space for small working groups to function effectively, both within and beyond the plenary hall, is now the most significant factor in selecting venues for the major assembly and synod meetings.

The wording of a proposal may undergo several changes before taking the form in which the council finally approves it. Insights gleaned in the course of discussion – perhaps sparked off by a previous speaker's contribution – may be included progressively by agreement of the meeting. So it is important that all participants are able to see at a glance, at any stage, the wording being considered. Data projection on a screen is helpful, as well as continuously upgraded overhead transparencies which achieve the same effect. Screens for viewing projected material, if that is what is relied on, must be clearly visible by all members of the council. This may mean extra large screens, or it may mean multiple screens displaying material from multiple projection points. Where electronic technology is not available, the chairperson must be careful to articulate clearly the final form of words before confirming that consensus has been reached. In smaller meetings, the chairperson or secretary may, from time to time, need to read out the wording that is agreed to that point, as well as immediately before a decision is finalized.

Similar attention needs to be given to ensuring that speakers can be heard clearly throughout the plenary hall. Emphasizing the importance of the contribution of all members, as consensus procedures are at pains to do, is pointless unless the facilities enable them readily to be heard when they do rise to speak.

When fluency in various languages differs, interpreters must also be briefed on the way the procedures are worked through and how the words of the final outcome are to be made clearly available to all before the matter is finalized. Where simultaneous interpretation is provided, a chairperson may need to pause to ensure the interpreters have communicated the final wording before declaring a consensus. Where electronic interpretation is not possible, sensitivity to the needs of members' language preferences is still important. Sometimes a personal interpreter sitting with a small group can facilitate understanding throughout the meeting. Where a speaker needs to use an interpreter to deliver a speech, appropriately extending the time available can be agreed by the meeting.

Minute-taking is challenging under consensus procedures. It's rather like holding a handful of dry sand, and feeling it slip between your fingers as you try to grasp it tighter! The words may just keep changing as the deliberations proceed. Clear communication between the person chairing and the recorder is essential. When it seems to the chairperson that the meeting is ready for consensus to be declared, the wording must be carefully checked with the recorder and preferably displayed before the meeting finally indicates its mind.

For a large gathering, attention should be given to equipping those with specific responsibilities:

- Those who will be called on to chair sessions need awareness and experience.
- Leaders of small groups need to be identified early and issued with some briefing on their role or required reading, prior to arrival at the venue. A training session on the first day with all small group leaders is often wise, particularly if some are inexperienced in the use of consensus procedures.
- A facilitation group will probably be necessary for a council with more than a hundred members, considering the number of small groups needed for everybody to be given an opportunity to voice their insights. This group also needs to be identified ahead of time, and carefully briefed on its role before and on arrival.
- Minute-takers need to be alerted to the extra demands put on them by consensus procedures, particularly the need for continual on-the-spot updating of proposal wording.

Contrary to widespread opinion both within the Uniting Church in Australia and beyond, the use of coloured indicator cards is not essential to a consensus model for meetings. The Uniting Church has found cards to be a novel tool for encouraging full participation in business meetings, for assisting awareness of the degree of support for ideas as they emerge, and for providing a more rapid way than counting hands when it comes to declaring an outcome. But a chairperson can seek indications in other ways: asking members to stand, or to raise a hand, or to respond with voices, are all quite legitimate means of discovering the mood of the meeting. And in more intimate settings, just glancing at each person in the circle for a nod or a shake of the head can quickly achieve the same awareness of whether consensus has been reached on an outcome.

No, the cards are not essential to functioning under consensus decision-making guidelines. But they certainly have been a useful innovation as well as fun to introduce! They have been significant when conveying the importance of every-member participation in consensus procedures. And undoubtedly they have been helpful in defusing any air of solemn formality that may threaten to stultify an attitude open to unexpected outcomes.

9. Where To Now?

It was using indicator cards that caught the imagination of the executive council of the World Alliance of Reformed Churches (WARC), meeting in Torre Pellice in northern Italy in July 2003. The executive was exploring the possibility of introducing consensus procedures for the WARC's 24th general council when it convenes in Accra, Ghana, in August 2004. A preparatory committee was aware of the fact that a number of WARC member churches were considering or experimenting with new models for meeting procedure. So it was looking seriously at whether introducing new procedures at the general council meeting might be both timely and appropriate.

Back in December 2002, a gathering hosted by the Reformed Church in America drew together representatives from eight or ten churches from North America and the Pacific region. All came with great interest in a more discerning model for meetings, and some with significant experience in new procedures. Experiences shared in that consultation revealed that a range of different approaches was being tested in different churches. A common theme to emerge was acknowledgment that adversarial procedures have resulted in polarized outcomes for contentious issues in all churches using them. They run counter to the conviction that Christians, together in community, are united in seeking God's will in finding answers to problems.

Charles Olsen, from the Presbyterian Church, USA, was the mentor for the consultation. In guiding the discussions, he brought a valued strong emphasis on a "worshipful work" approach to decision-making councils of the church.[1] This attitude of a more spiritual approach to business was reflected in the reports of each of the participants, all of them emphasizing their church's desire to find clearer guidelines for discerning God's will when making decisions.

Those present at the Princeton consultation agreed that a consensus model (or discernment model, as some prefer to

---

1 Danny Morris and Charles Olsen, *Discerning God's Will Together*, Bethesda MD, Alban Institute, 1997.

call a similar process) is more likely to create an atmosphere helpful for change. And a change in members' approach to their work might enable greater awareness of the Spirit's guidance, greater participation in deliberations and greater ownership of outcomes. The transitional phase for churches that have tested some change in procedures has not been without awkwardness and resentment, of course, but caution and defensiveness have not diminished a strong commitment to persevere in developing more appropriate models for meetings.

WARC's Torre Pellice experience

Aware of such stirrings afoot in many churches, the WARC general council preparatory committee invited the Uniting Church in Australia to assist them in investigating the ramifications of changing procedures for the general council meeting. Accordingly, I was with them in Italy in July 2003 to introduce the consensus concept, to share something of the Uniting Church's experience, and to join with them in considering how the procedures might be adapted to meet the needs of the general council in session.

Through circulated briefing papers and on-the-spot presentations to both preparatory committee and executive council, we considered the Australian church's processes and the theological basis for consensus procedures, and canvassed some thoughts on considerations for Accra. But it was the use of the blue and orange indicator cards in the general business sessions of the meeting which really helped members start to experience what it might be like to work by consensus rather than by formal majority procedures. A glimpse of the liberating potential in changing to more flexible meeting procedures started to catch the imagination of both members and those moderating the sessions alike.

A consensus model for decision-making was tried out in plenary sessions for the two weeks of the Torre Pellice meetings. At the end of that time, the executive council agreed to adopt new procedures for the general council in Accra, procedures which will reflect better its purposes in community-building and discernment of God's will for the council. Although based on the demonstrated consensus procedures, the new procedures will be called a "discernment model", because members were conscious of a number of conflicting understandings about the use of the term "consensus" from their different cultural backgrounds. It was agreed that the new guidelines to be developed would open up the rules of procedure to allow for greater flexibility, increased participation, and "less tedious and technical debates".

Being conscious of the particular challenges of a multicultural, multi-lingual, multi-denominational gathering, the executive council decided to move cautiously, initially introducing a temporary transitional model. The agenda will be structured according to consensus principles, but voting cards as well as indicator cards will be used throughout, and the meeting will retain simple majority voting as the final point in decision-making. Once the experience of the new procedures in Accra is reviewed and analyzed, the executive council is open to continuing the journey towards discovering more effective ways of conducting business sessions.

Individual churches may be struggling to introduce change in their meeting procedures smoothly, in a way that is acceptable to their councils and membership. But theirs is nothing like the dilemma encountered by an international ecumenical organization! The complexities are enormous in considering meeting structure for a council comprising many different churches, from many different cultures and language groups, and with background familiarity in many different models of meeting procedure.

Progress in the World Council of Churches

The World Council of Churches (WCC) is in the process of walking a parallel tortuous pathway – perhaps even more complex than the WARC's because of the broader theological spectrum found in the churches in membership with the WCC.

The eighth assembly of the WCC, meeting in Harare, Zimbabwe, in December 1998, agreed to appoint a special commission on Orthodox participation in the WCC, with a broad agenda addressing a number of concerns and criticisms arising from the Orthodox churches' membership and involvement. The purpose was to recommend changes to the structure, style and ethos of the Council, and to restore mutuality and trust among the membership. After nearly four years of the special commission's work, the central committee of the WCC adopted a range of proposals in August-September 2002.

One group of those proposals, arising from the meticulous work of the broadly based special commission, concerned decision-making processes. The commission proposed that consensus procedures should be introduced by the WCC. The main reasons for this recommendation were to "enhance the participation of all members in the various meetings", to "preserve the rights of all churches, especially those which hold a minority opinion", and to "provide a more collaborative and harmonious context for the making of decisions". The experience of a number of WCC member churches was taken into account in reaching this conclusion. D'Arcy Wood, a former president of the Uniting Church in Australia, was a member of the special commission. He contributed significant insight from his experience of the work of the Australian church, particularly in formulating the theological basis and the possible steps to be considered in any change in the WCC procedures.

The 2002 decision of the central committee to move to a consensus model of decision-making was taken, according to the general secretary Konrad Raiser, "recognizing the spirit of mutual trust and commitment to discerning the mind of Christ, and respecting the diversity that underlies the special commission's proposal". It was noted that many of the member churches of the WCC, contrary to the situation in 1948 when the Council was founded, now are from cultures where Westminster-style parliamentary procedures are quite foreign. This would be true particularly for churches in Africa and for most of the Orthodox churches. It was also acknowledged that the means by which churches search for a common mind is as important as the decisions they reach, and that the mandate of a WCC assembly is "spiritual and ecclesial rather than juridical and political".

The exciting decision of the central committee to introduce changed procedures was of course a beginning point, not the end of the journey for the WCC. Since then, thorough exploration of potential problems and possible transition points has been exercising the minds of a skilled implementation committee, along with clarification of policy issues. The WCC has embarked on an adventurous pathway which needs to be trodden with extreme care and sensitivity, and which will undoubtedly require time and patience before the goal is reached. The complex structures currently in place for meetings of both central committee and assembly have been entrenched for a long time, and to change what is the established norm does require prudence and fortitude. The intention is to have a draft version of revised rules and an explanatory manual prepared in time for testing at the central committee meeting in February 2005. Full implementation is expected to be in place for the ninth assembly in Porto Alegre, Brazil, in 2006.

As with the experience of the Uniting Church in Australia, there will be those representatives and member churches of the WCC who await the outcome of the journey with relief and joyful anticipation. There also will be those who are suspicious, or dread the thought of coping with a different design for doing business. But the motivation for the change, according to Konrad Raiser, is the undergirding conviction that a representative gathering of a fellowship of Christian churches should be prepared to be exposed to the guidance of the Spirit in seeking to discern the will of God.

There's risk in that conviction. But there's also an invitation to experience exhilarating liberation!

Personal reflection

I rejoice that the introduction of consensus procedures for councils of the Uniting Church in Australia occurred during my time as national president of the church (1994-97). Challenging as it certainly was, it remains the major highlight of my term of office. In every meeting I chair, there's a growing sense of awe at how openness to the unexpected in seeking a way forward for the church can be such an enriching spiritual experience. My conviction about the rightness of the change has not diminished over the years of involvement with consensus procedures, in spite of some disappointments at the fact that it may not have been used to fullest advantage in some councils of our church.

Yet I was one of those who wielded the previous adversarial-style rules of debate with enthusiasm and efficacy. I had previously presided over councils of the Uniting Church in Australia at every level of the church's governance, and also served a term as president of one of our state ecumenical councils of churches. I knew and used with confidence the complex formal majority procedures that were the former standing orders and rules of debate. As a participant in church meetings beyond number for more than half a century, I have revelled in the cut-and-thrust of deft application of formal procedures to achieve a predetermined outcome. I have known again and again the thrill of winning in achieving the outcome desired in debate, as powerful an adrenaline rush as in any sport.

So there is a feeling of some shame as I look back now, in the light of our very different experience of the years since 1994. I now can recognize my (at times) shallow disregard in the past for tentative voices not as adept as I in meeting procedure. I now can see there were occasions when others must have felt diminished by my way of "winning" in a debate. I now can appreciate there is a better way – a way that is more honouring of my faith and my convictions about Christian community. The Quakers tell us that "process marks the religious path, not the end achievement". I'm beginning to glimpse a little of what that means. And I think the Uniting Church in Australia has taken some steps towards more faithfully defining such a pathway in the fellowship of our faith community in the councils of the church.

These consensus procedures are far from perfect. I hope we will continue to learn from the experience of other churches and councils of churches about different approaches that may enhance our goals. Yet, imperfect as they are, I do see – even in what we have in place now – a potential for lifting our horizons beyond some of the polarizing attitudes of the past. I do see a hope for a genuine possibility of greater unity within the life of the church, as we join with integrity in seeking to discern God's will for the way forward.

Any procedures can be only the servant of those who use them. Is it presumptuous to assume that each of us who participates in the decision-making life of the church, at whatever level, fervently desires to follow the Lord of the church? Is it too much to expect that each of us will translate that desire into action, in the way we participate in the discernment process? Is it possible we might actually look forward to discerning something of God's will through voices with quite contrary points of view to our own?

Throughout the world at this time, we are part-way through celebrating the WCC's Decade to Overcome Violence: Churches Seeking Reconciliation and Peace (2001-10). The message we are affirming in the Decade is that in Jesus Christ there is hope, there is life, and there is a way for peace to prevail. That hope, that life, that way, is one of reconciliation, of breaking down barriers, of healing for old wounds.

My prayer is that the message of peace which we proclaim to the world and with which we challenge the churches throughout this Decade and beyond may also be experienced to the full as we model it in our church meetings.

Appendix 1

Members of the Task Group

The members of te task group on standing orders and rules of debate were as follows:

Mrs Tricia Lewis (convenor to December 1989)
Rev. John Rowland (convenor from April 1990)
Rev. Hamish Christie-Johnstone
Mr Geoffrey Grinton
Mr Mike Smith (from April 1990)
Mr Frank Wright
Miss Kate Graham (to April 1990)
Mrs Alison Ingamells (April-August 1990)
Rev. Laurie Turner (to March 1989)

Ex-officio:
Rev. Gregor Henderson (assembly general secretary during this period)
Dr Jill Tabart (assembly president-elect July 1991-June 1994)

Appendix 2
Consensus Procedures

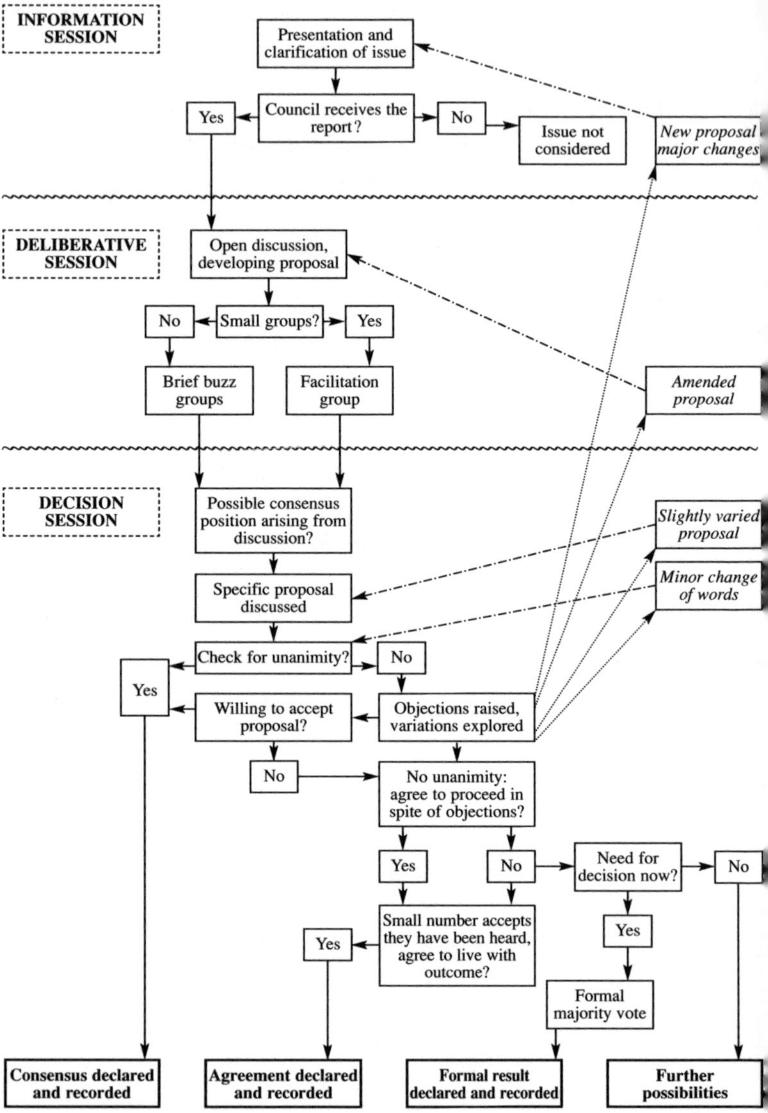

Flow chart taken from *A Manual for Meetings 2000*, UCA, 2001. Used with permission.

Appendix 3
Formal Majority Procedures

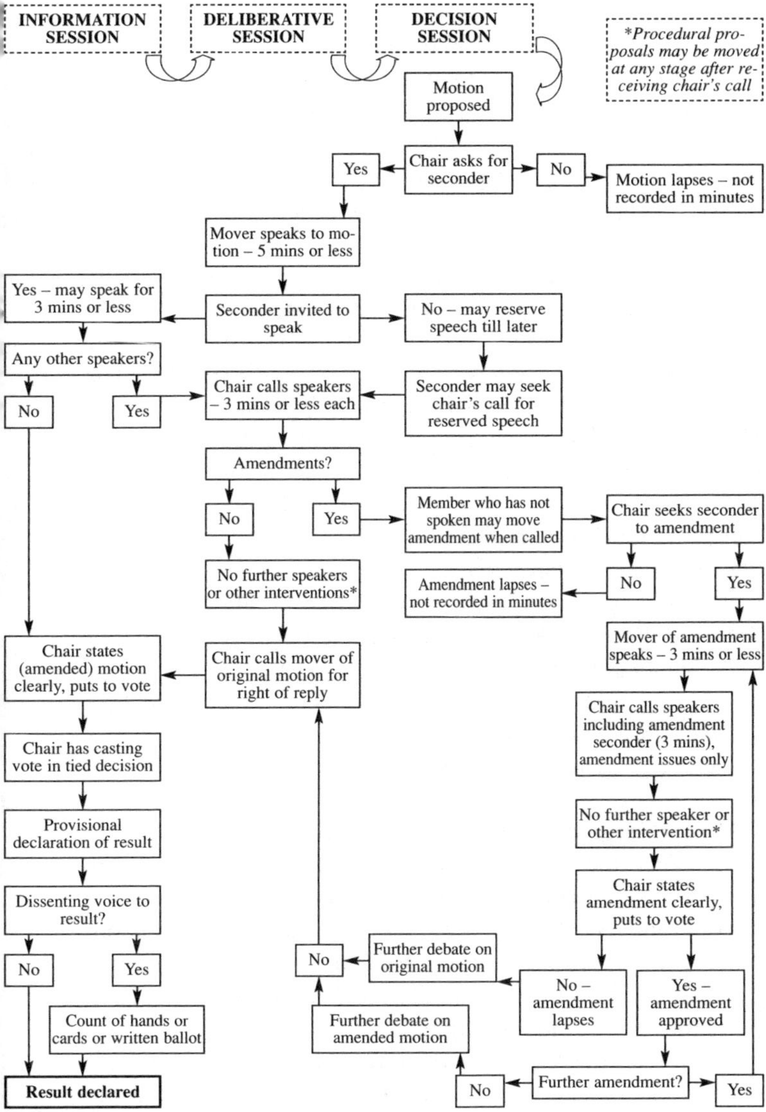

Flow chart taken from *A Manual for Meetings 2000*, UCA, 2001. Used with permission.

Appendix 4

Consensus Decision-Making

Foreword

This appendix has its own history. In its original form it was a background paper to assist the discussion of the Special Commission on the issue of decision-making. In this form, it argued the case for change to existing decision-making processes and described the consensus model as an alternative process – or, to be more precise, one form of the consensus model.

As the Special Commission has continued its work, many comments have been made on the paper, and the Special Commission has made decisions which have now become recommendations to the central committee of the WCC. The paper has therefore been revised and expanded considerably. However, it still bears the marks of its original purpose, namely as background material. In its revised form – as an appendix to the final report of the Special Commission – it serves as rationale, description and elaboration not only of the reasons for change but of the character of the proposed methods of decision-making. If the proposals are accepted by the central committee, the next step would be (1) to redraft the relevant portions of the rules of the WCC, and (2) to institute a transition process, whereby moderators and members of governing bodies can be helped to enter into the new procedures confidently and effectively.

I. Why change decision-making procedures?

1. When the World Council of Churches was founded in 1948 the great majority of member churches were located in Europe and North America. The procedures for decision-making were, not unnaturally, based on the procedures customarily used in church councils – and secular bodies such as parliaments – in those continents.

2. In the intervening years more and more churches have become members. For many of the churches, especially

---

• This text is appendix B to the report of the Special Commission on Orthodox Participation in the WCC, which was adopted by the WCC central committee in August-September 2002.

Orthodox, these procedures do not resonate with the procedures of their own churches, or even, in some cases, with the cultures from which they come. There are differences, for example, between North and South. So the question is raised as to whether the current procedures should continue in their present form.

3. A second issue is the adversarial nature of the procedures. Proposals are debated "for and against". While amendments are possible – and frequent – speakers are encouraged to argue in favour or against, rather than to explore. On many issues there are of course three or four different viewpoints, not just two. While there is provision for questions concerning any proposals, the adversarial nature of the process is still apparent. In some cultures this adversarial approach, which can even be confrontational, is something to be avoided. Further, it is arguable that the church, being the body of Christ, is true to its inner nature when it is exploratory, seeking the mind of Christ and striving after a consensus which can declare: "it seemed good to the Holy Spirit and to us..." (Acts 15:28). Rather than striving to succeed in debate, our aim should be a mutual submission, seeking to "understand what the will of the Lord is" (Eph. 5:17).

4. A third issue is the method of voting. In the present system a majority of 50 percent plus one is sufficient for a proposal to carry, unless some special provision is made for a different percentage. Many matters are not closely related to doctrine or ecclesiology, and on these the voting will not usually follow denominational or cultural or geographical lines. But on other matters there has been, especially in recent years, a difference of approach between Orthodox on the one hand and Protestants, Anglicans and Old Catholics on the other. Other combinations are of course possible, but with the present system of representation and membership (which is addressed elsewhere in the Special Commission's report) the Orthodox are a minority in the governing bodies of the WCC and in certain cases have been outvoted. The proliferation of small member churches also affects the nature of the Council. The question of reform of "voting power" may be part of

the solution, but in this part of our report the issue is the voice of minorities and how that voice can best be reflected in the decisions that are made. Not only Orthodox participants in the WCC but other churches as well experience frustration at their inability to influence decisions sufficiently.

5. The fourth in this list of reasons is the rigidity of meeting procedures, not only in the WCC but in many church bodies. The system of motions, amendments, further amendments, points of order and so on, while it can certainly work well with some matters and on some occasions, often seems inappropriate to the complex questions of true Christian obedience, of proper ecumenical relations, and of a Christian approach to historical, social and global change. Procedures which allow more room for consultation, exploration, questioning and prayerful reflection would be likely to promote the purposes of the WCC better than the formal and often rigid procedures that are currently used. Even when it is doing its "business", the church should seek to express that faith which is "made effective through love" (Gal. 5:6). This is not to say that the WCC should attempt to do without rules: on the contrary, rules that are fair, readily understood and workable are essential. The question is the style, content and application of such rules.

6. In 1 Corinthians 12:12-27 St Paul speaks of parts of the body needing each other. A fully functioning body integrates the abilities and contributions of all the members. So it is in the church. A set of procedures which makes the best possible use of the abilities, the history, the experience, the commitment and the spiritual tradition of all the member churches should be the aim of the WCC.

7. If changes are made, they should be formulated after wide consultation. And once introduced, they may still be modified in the light of further experience. The Orthodox principle of *oikonomia* would suggest that the ecumenical movement can accommodate change and development as the issues and circumstances change. While the principle of *oikonomia* [economy: flexibility in making a decision and enforcing it] has been applied, historically, mainly to the

sacraments, it can also refer to right judgment in other ecclesial matters – always, of course, in the light of faith. To respect the *oikonomia* is to be open to various expressions of faith and life while remaining true to the "faith that was once for all entrusted to the saints" (Jude 3). The experience of all traditions represented in the WCC is valuable and should be utilized, as and where practical, in the common life, the functioning and the programmes of the Council.

II. What sort of change? A possible direction

8. A method of decision-making based on consensus may well overcome most of the difficulties identified above. This document explores consensus decision-making with the hope that it can be adopted by the WCC for all levels of governance. The consensus method is a means of arriving at decisions without voting. It is more conciliar than parliamentary, and more inclusive than adversarial. Some Orthodox churches use a similar procedure, also some other churches such as the Religious Society of Friends and the Uniting Church in Australia. The experience of these churches is reflected in the following summary; however no particular model can be simply transferred from a denominational context to the ecumenical context of the WCC: adaptations will be needed.

9. It should be noted, first, that consensus is not the same as unanimity (see §14 below). For example, a minority may agree to let a proposal go forward which has convinced the majority but not the minority, i.e. the minority accepts that the proposal represents the general "mind of the meeting". This becomes possible when a minority feels that its concerns have been heard, understood and respected.

10. It is possible, too, to include, within the WCC rules, a provision that some matters will be decided by majority vote, either a simple majority or a greater number. In other words, consensus would be the normal procedure but not the invariable procedure. At the beginning of a session, the moderator would indicate clearly the procedures that operate in that ses-

sion. The rules would determine those items of business which will be determined by vote.

11. How then does consensus procedure work? Typically a proposal, not always in complete or final form, is put forward, following which open discussion rather than "debate" begins. Usually the proposal has already been refined by a committee (see end of this section). The discussion may include questions. Members of the meeting may speak more than once. It is up to the moderator to ensure that all who wish to speak can do so and that no individual or small group dominates the discussion to the exclusion of others. It is important that all relevant views are brought forward at this exploratory stage.

12. As discussion continues, anyone may propose a change to the proposal without having to move an amendment. The moderator should test the response of the meeting to any such idea or modification by calling for an expression of opinion (sometimes called a "straw vote"). As the proposal continues to be discussed, the moderator needs to sense when the meeting is close to agreement. She or he may need to allow extra time for various denominational or cultural views to be expressed, but at an appropriate time the moderator should ask the meeting: "Are we agreed on this matter?" Or (similarly): "How many of you could accept this proposal in its current form?" This frequent testing of the mind of the meeting is central to the development of a consensus.

13. The assembly or committee may send a proposal to a drafting group or it may divide the whole meeting into subgroups for a short or longer time, the purpose being to generate further refinements of the ideas and thereby move the meeting closer to consensus. "Table groups" or other groupings are also useful in clearing up misunderstandings. A weighty matter would typically be considered over several sessions, with time in between for a committee to incorporate comments and concerns from the discussion.

14a. A consensus is reached, then, when any *one* of the following occurs:

1. all are in agreement (unanimity);
2. most are in agreement and those who disagree are content that the discussion has been both full and fair and that the proposal expresses the general "mind of the meeting"; the minority therefore gives consent;
3. the meeting acknowledges that there are various opinions, and it is agreed that these be recorded in the body of the proposal (not just in the minutes);
4. it is agreed that the matter be postponed;
5. it is agreed that no decision can be reached.

14b. Therefore, consensus procedures allow any family or other group of churches, through a spokesperson, to have their objections to any proposal addressed and satisfied prior to the adoption of the proposal. This implies that the family or group of churches can stop any proposal from passing until they are satisfied that their concerns have been fully addressed.

15a. If consensus *cannot* be reached, certain questions should be asked, such as:

1. "Must a decision on this matter be made today?" If not, the matter should be deferred to a later session (tomorrow, next week, or some other time). Further seasoning by a committee and informal discussion among those with strong views will often bring the meeting to a different level of agreement at a later session. If yes (and this is quite rare), the attention of the meeting must shift from approving or not approving the proposal at hand to finding other ways of meeting the pressing or time-critical need. Interim solutions can sometimes be found while the meeting searches for consensus on the original question.
2. "Can this proposal be acted upon, on the understanding that some members (or member churches) cannot support it?" If no, the proposal should be deferred for further work, as above. If yes, the effect is that those persons, or member churches, or parts of the Council, being of a dissenting opinion, nevertheless allow a policy or programme to go forward without endorsing it. This is sometimes called "standing aside". In social and political

issues it may sometimes be appropriate for some member churches or some committee or agency of the WCC to speak without committing the Council as a whole to one point of view (cf. the group in the Special Commission dealing with methodology in social and political matters).

3. "Have we asked the right question?" When agreement on the issue, as posed, is not possible, this should not be regarded as failure. Sometimes a different question will yield a consensus. Sometimes it is helpful to ask "what can we say together?" The meeting may not be of one mind on a particular statement on a difficult issue, but may find great value in articulating its various perspectives and the fruits of its discussion. There may be foundational principles on which we all agree. A clear articulation of these, followed by a description of the diverse conclusions that Christians of good conscience have reached, can be a powerful product of a discussion.

15b. In rare situations, if the consensus procedures have been tried and have not succeeded, a mechanism will be needed to remove the blockage. The rules should specify how this emergency provision operates, ensuring that the emergency provision does not weaken the consensus procedures themselves. When drawing up this rule, consultation with the proposed standing committee (§21 below) should take place.

16. In all cases in which consensus proves elusive, it is incumbent on those with concerns to work closely with those who initiated the item of business so as to find creative ways of moving forward. A major purpose of the WCC is for churches to learn from each other, to deepen their fellowship and to be better equipped for their mission. This means that there will be occasions when the churches accept a situation of disagreement while continuing to help and support each other.

17. It can be gauged from the above description that effective chairing is essential to the success of consensus procedures. The moderator must be fair, sensitive and experienced. She or he must be able to sense the trend of a dis-

cussion and help the meeting to crystallize its thinking. Misunderstandings can be avoided if the moderator "checks" frequently the development of the mind of the meeting. This can be done, for example, by the use of coloured cards (say, orange for a positive opinion, blue for a negative). Such opinion can be sought on a part of a proposal, even a small part. The moderator can help the meeting by asking a "blue card holder" to explain what it is that prevents him or her from giving assent to the ideas being put forward. In this way objections can be aired, and possibly dealt with, as the discussion evolves. The aim is for the meeting as a whole to participate in developing the final decision, i.e. not only those who are particularly adept in debate, or those who use the official languages easily, or those who put the proposal forward in the first place. The rules should specify the role of moderators. While flexibility is important, it is also necessary to give guidelines for chairing meetings.

18. Between sittings the moderator may use a moderatorial group or reference group to provide advice. A business committee may perform the same function.

19. It is advisable, in an extended meeting, to specify the type of procedure for each particular session, e.g. a "voting" session, a "consensus" discussion, an "information" session. Such clear delineation may help members, especially the newer ones, or those working in their second, third or fourth language to participate more easily. If the procedure is changed during a session, this should be done with care and with full explanation. If a complex or contentious issue is to be dealt with, prior notice is important. Prior to the actual discussion, i.e. at an earlier session, it can be helpful to give a "preview" of the issue so as to help members in their discussion at a later time.

20. The above principles, outlined only briefly here, need converting into rules. When these rules have been adopted and put into practice, experience over the months and years will indicate where further modifications need to be made. There is no single or pure form of the consensus method: the aim should be to develop a specific form for the specific

needs of the WCC and to adjust the procedures in the light of experience. The Orthodox principle of oikonomia is relevant here. If the purposes of the WCC and of its programmes and policies are clear, the means by which these purposes, programmes and policies are achieved can be reviewed whenever it is desirable to do so.

21. In the work of the Special Commission, further suggestions which do not belong exactly to the consensus principles have been made. The first of these is the establishment of a standing committee on Orthodox participation. The detailed proposal is in the final report of the Special Commission. The principle of parity is important here.

22. The second is that if modifications to particular proposals have been prepared before a meeting sits, these should be notified – even circulated before the meeting begins – so as to allow adequate time for reflection. This would especially help those who are new or those who are working in a language which is not their first language. This provision implies that sudden changes to proposals (in the older terminology "late amendments") should be permitted only when there is adequate time for explanation and discussion.

23. A third suggestion is that business committees should prepare for a plenary session in such a way as to avoid unnecessary polarizing of opinion. Such committees may also be called between sessions of a meeting to advise on procedure and to interpret the progress of the meeting. The concerns of minorities can sometimes be conveyed through members of a group such as this. When sensitive issues of ecclesiology or of a moral or political nature are proposed for discussion, the preparation by such a committee can help to ensure justice for all parties and also help avoid divisive debate. The rules of the WCC already describe the work of business committees, and these rules may need review. A business committee should where possible follow consensus procedures.

24. The keeping of minutes is an important task. The meeting needs to understand what it is agreeing to, so the text of all decisions should be read or displayed during the meet-

ing. Major contributions to any discussion should also be recorded and this should include a summary of differing viewpoints. The right for a minority to have its dissent recorded in the minutes and/or in any report of the meeting should be preserved, although in consensus procedures it is rare for such a right to be exercised. Sometimes it will be helpful for a small group to review the minutes before they are issued.

III. Possible difficulties with the consensus procedure

25. It has been suggested that the consensus procedure can be cumbersome and slow. For example, a published chart which outlines the Uniting Church in Australia's version of the procedure looks quite complicated. There are numerous steps to take on the way to declaring a consensus.

26. However, the experience of churches which use the consensus method indicates that this fear is probably exaggerated. Because people are working in a system which is less adversarial and less rigid than the older procedures, participants seem more prepared to listen to alternative views and to accept differences of opinion. It is not the case that the procedures, in normal circumstances, retard the making of decisions. Some discussions may be slow-moving, certainly, but this may be desirable if the topic requires detailed exploration or if there is a divergence of viewpoint. Generally there is an increased sense of cooperation simply because of the flexible and collaborative nature of the process. It should be admitted that, under consensus procedures, fewer decisions may sometimes flow from a particular meeting, the reason being that careful consultation takes time.

27. A second possible difficulty is that minorities – even one or two individuals – can stand in the way of forward-looking or innovative proposals. In other words, the desire for full participation and for consensus could open the door to unnecessary delay or even obstruction in the consideration of new ideas.

28. The response to this is twofold. First, consensus is not the same as unanimity. While everyone in a meeting can con-

tribute to discussion, there is usually no voting. Objectors (we could call them "blue card holders") can state their objections but the moderator will seek their concurrence with the wishes of a clear majority of the meeting. In this way no-one's conscience is compromised, and decisions can still be made in an orderly way.

29. The other response is about the psychology of consensus procedure. While blue card holders have the right for their dissent to be recorded in the minutes and/or in any report of the meeting, experience shows that they rarely insist on this. The reason is that the discussion allows for many contributions and the moderator is responsible for seeing that the discussion has been both fair and as detailed as it needs to be. Because minorities are not "squashed", their response is normally to allow the meeting to move ahead to a decision.

30. Thirdly, it has been suggested that the "prophetic voice" of the WCC could be muted by the checks and balances of the consensus model. Again there are two points to be made in response. First, the encouragement of open discussion actually allows a diversity of views to be expressed. Second, the care taken in reaching decisions promotes the "owning" by all members of a meeting and therefore the solidarity of the ecumenical fellowship. Where decisions are not unanimous, and even where consensus proves to be unreachable, there is a process of reflection and enrichment which strengthens the voice of the Council. A document which honestly explores the diversity of opinion within the ecumenical community can be a profoundly "prophetic" expression. To face differences squarely, and to accept each other in Christian love, is important in any ecumenical body.

31. A fourth possible difficulty is the amount of power given to the moderator. She or he must guide the discussion, sum up from time to time, and perceive when a consensus is developing. This responsibility is great, and (as in any procedures) mistakes can be made. But the flexible nature of the procedures is an effective balance to this heavy responsibility of the chair, i.e. any member of the meeting, without hav-

ing to move "dissent from the ruling of the chair" (or some similar motion), can make a suggestion at any time concerning the guiding of the meeting. A good moderator (as in any procedures) will be open to suggestions. As soon as any member is dissatisfied with the handling of the business, a remedy is at hand. Some examples of such remedies have been given above. A reference group or business committee could also advise the moderator regarding the efficient handling of the business (see §23).

32. It has been suggested that a process of equipping moderators for their new role may be advisable. This is because the change of procedure to a consensus model is more than a technical matter or a change of rules. Members of a meeting, as well as moderators, need to adopt a different attitude towards decision-making. A "transition plan" should be developed, and perhaps a handbook issued.

IV. Conclusion

33. The above paper gives a description of how consensus procedures work, and the benefits that can be gained. To convert the principles into rules is a further step. It is important to reach agreement (even a consensus!) about the aims and principles first, and then to translate the principles into actual procedures suitable to the needs of the WCC.

34. The principles described above are an attempt to implement the accepted ecumenical aim of enabling all representatives and member churches to be heard within a committed fellowship which accepts differences of theology, culture and ecclesial tradition. Minorities may express their mind on any issue, and should, in consensus procedures, be allowed more than one attempt, if needed, to explain the basis of their views. At the same time the WCC can still (as it must) make the decisions about policy and programmes which are essential to its life.

35. All churches believe in the centrality of holy scripture in their life and doctrine. A significant image of the church in the New Testament is the image of the body of Christ, diverse and yet one. In the life of the WCC, with its funda-

mental aim of promoting the unity of all Christians, there must similarly be respect for diversity and difference. The rules and procedures which govern the working of the Council should enshrine this respect. While ecclesiologies in the WCC differ considerably from one tradition to another, the life of the Council should as far as possible be a mirror of the essential nature of the church. The consensus procedures offer an opportunity for the Council to put into practice a model of unity, a respect for diversity and the making of decisions in a way that is careful, flexible, frank and unifying.

Appendix 5

Helpful Resources

Dicker, Gordon S., *Faith with Understanding* (rev. ed.), Melbourne, JBCE, 1996.

Johnson, Luke Timothy, *Scripture and Discernment: Decision Making in the Church*, Nashville, Abingdon Press, 1983.

A Manual for Meetings 2000, Uniting Church in Australia, obtainable at http://www.mediacomonline.org.au/uc01/

Morris, Danny E. and Olsen, Charles M., *Discerning God's Will Together*, Bethesda MD, Alban Institute, 1997.

Olsen, Charles M., *Transforming Church Boards into Communities of Spiritual Leaders*, Bethesda MD, Alban Institute, 1995.

Uniting Church in Australia: http://www.uca.org.au

Appendix 6

Glossary of Terms

assembly:
the national council of the UCA, comprising lay and ordained representatives from each synod and presbytery

assembly agency:
body responsible for a specific area of work of the UCA nationally

church council:
the local council of the UCA, elected from within the congregation

council of the church:
a church council (local), a presbytery (regional), a synod (state/territory) or the assembly (national)

member:
a person entitled to participate in a council of the UCA; also used to denote a baptized member of the church

presbytery:
one of 52 regional councils of the UCA, comprising lay and ordained representatives of congregations within its bounds

standing orders and rules of debate:
the formal meeting procedures of the UCA used until 1994

synod:
one of 6 (7 until 2002) state/territory-based councils of the UCA, comprising representatives from each of the presbyteries within its bounds

UCA:
Uniting Church in Australia